GANGRILLAS

GANGRILLAS
The Unspoken
Pros and Cons of Legalizing Drugs

D. Méndez Beddow
and
Sam J. Thibodeaux

Order this book online at www.trafford.com
or email orders@trafford.com

Most Trafford titles are also available at major online book retailers.

Printed in the United States of America.

ISBN: 978-1-4269-4846-6 (sc)
ISBN: 978-1-4269-4847-3 (e)

Gangrillas: The unspoken pros and cons of legalizing drugs
Author: D. Mendez Beddow
Co-Author: Sam J. Thibodeaux
Claim ID: 1 - 89ESDZ
Case #: 1 - 499535911
Case Details Reference: 1 -89ESG7

Library of Congress Control Number: 2010917019

Trafford rev. 11/30/2010

 www.trafford.com

North America & international
toll-free: 1 888 232 4444 (USA & Canada)
phone: 250 383 6864 ♦ fax: 812 355 4082

To Charlie and our Angels

INDEX

PREFACE

Simon Bolívar's idea to integrate the Western Hemispheric nations as a united group has acquired momentum in Latin America with a twisted version that synergizes China, North Korea, Iran and Russia towards a nuclear proliferation process. Our theoretical model explores how imminent trends indicate this emerging model of "Bolivarización," or "Bolivarization," may adversely affect the national security of the United States of America, and hemispheric stability, if it is fully implemented based on the indicators available through leading actors of this process. Narco-terrorist groups representative of disruptive revolutionary movements in the region have been provided with weapons and supplies during the initial stages of the "Bolivarización" process. An increased acquisition of weapons, equipment, and military aircrafts in preparation for an "invasion" by the USA has been used as an excuse for proliferation. Early inclusion of China to provide "technical advisors" in the region, along with open rhetorical attacks against US–Latin American policies, send a dynamic message to investigate the repercussions associated to regional security and, specifically, the national security of the United States of America.

Gang activities in major cities throughout the Western Hemisphere, sudden massive demonstrations of militant illegal immigrants, diplomatic relations between narco-terrorist groups and *de juro* governments, as well as the fact that terrorist sleeper cells momentum has failed to materialize demands urgent research. Emerging unification of similar actors from Asia and the Middle East, whose common denominator to some Latin

American countries is a global effort to adulterate democratic systems, has become a core challenge.

The link between different magnets in the Western Hemisphere are researched in an effort to determine a vertical alignment of rhetorical threats, negotiations and agreements that may serve as indicators of terrorist events promoted under the emerging movement called "Bolivarización." Latin America's sudden fascination with "socialist democratic" governments is the financial result of great investments in gathering the Western Hemisphere under one umbrella. Simon Bolivar has served as inspiration to façade presidents like Fidel Castro and Hugo Chavez, who contradictorily consider themselves a reincarnation of the great liberator. The upsurge of elected "socialist-democratic" dictators has climaxed with a hemispheric union that has created a global army of the most bizarre characters. Their determination has proven to be a successful enterprise in its theoretical and implementation stages.

On Friday, April 30, 2010 we walked into our home and the phone was ringing. The call from an impossible mission shed the light on the epidemic known as the "Gangrillas." Incredibly, illegal drug trade is providing the funding that makes a success of this bizarre concoction. Hopefully, the Southwestern and coastal states in the United States of America will provide the antibiotic tonics to protect a nation under attack. The rest of our nation will hold on its shoulders the responsibility for controlling the most outrageous *de facto* underworld government of narcoterrorism. Will the "Gangrillas" succeed? Is legalizing drugs our answer? **Your** answer to this call is urgent!

CHAPTER I

Illegal drugs: Pros and Cons of Legalization:

Will the process of legalization force skyrocketing drug prices due to taxation and production regulations?

The United States of America has waged a war on drugs for nearly half a century, which cost the taxpayers an insurmountable amount of cash and lives. It has generated a continuous renewal system of initiatives driven to help underground organizations to overcome all the measures imaginable created by governments. It has driven developing nations to create attractive financial systems complex enough to deter international anti-narcotic measures for decades. Nevertheless, nations involved in legalization of drugs have encountered the same frustration levels we face. A look at any recognized system capable of managing the use of illegal drugs without punishment results in a nightmare of laws to protect legalization capable of convincing the growers, middlemen, cartels, dealers, and drug addicts that maintaining drugs at an illegal level punishable by law enforcement agencies is a better option than legalization.

Illegal drug trade in the Western Hemisphere is probably the most capitalist profitable business available to men and women at all levels of the educational and financial spectrum. It engages and affects society indiscriminately, creating the most effective marketing strategy at a transnational level. Disruption of the near perfect illegal systems generated and refined for decades by cartels, middlemen, farmers, and all the corrupt politicians and businessmen associated to this successful enterprise will result in the most devastating economic collapse at the global level. The

1

legalization of any type of illegal drugs in the United States of America will force this complex socio-political-economic network into a down ward spiral deterioration capable of producing massive bankruptcy at all social levels around the world. The benefits to our society may not provide the relief expected through legalization.

COCA LEAF PRODUCTS

We would like to look at the process on a step-by-step basis that would begin with hard core drugs such as cocaine. The countries producing coca leaves are mostly developing nations that depend on the subterranean economy generated by illegal drugs. Taking Bolivia and Peru as an example will lead us to the basic production levels, which begin with the farmers. Evo Morales, president of Bolivia, considers himself a "cocalero," a productive child from a family that survived economically thanks to coca leaves illegal farming production. The capitalist enterprise that nurtured, subsidized, and supported an illegal crop farmer from the Andean farm to the national presidency is now rejected in behalf of reform capable of legalizing coca leaves production under a socialized government. Although it is likely for the government of Bolivia to legalize the production of coca, its impact will force counterproductive measures at a regional level. These measures will prevent Andean indigenous populations from achieving power using the financial opportunities available through illegal drug trade.

Peru and Bolivia have provided the raw material, coca, at the lowest level of the crack-cocaine marketing production. The profit margins for these countries are the lowest in the illegal drug business. Mass legalized production of the raw material will likely force its value to a decrease in the marketing profit to the subterranean economy. Instead of increasing the per capita income for the coca farming community, Evo Morales is actually proposing a decrease in income levels for the very same industry that provided the funding and resources responsible for his rise to power. Legalizing production will actually encourage the large landowners to enter the new business venture and mass produce coca leaves. The overproduction of coca will result in a decline of its selling price due to competition. Distribution of wealth under a legalized political system would result on an equal distribution of poverty at the hands of political and business bureaucratic control.

The opportunities available to generate the cash crop would become taxable under a legalized system. It would be foreseeable that engaging in the legal coca leaf production will degenerate in a capitalist process that will control and decrease the cash flow available to the indigenous farming community in developing nations.

In the event that the global community decided to legalize drugs, after recognizing and accepting the production of illegal crops, new debates would arise on the quality of this agricultural raw material. The industry would be inclined to establish a series of demands on the conditions under which the material is produced. This would impose new standards upon a largely uneducated community. Requirements would have to be imposed at government levels to control transnational trade, which in turn would engrain bureaucratic networks.

Growth of coca leaves requires a certain level of humidity at determined sea level heights. The climate conditions needed to nurture coca leaf production are unique to the Andean region, although attempts have been made to grow the crop in other geographical areas closely resembling the Andes. Understanding the nature of transnational corporations is an important factor to recognize in our quest to determine if legalization of this crop will benefit or hurt the different social levels engaged in the industry. It would be clear, though, that control at a globalized legal level will overexpose and undermine the needs of the farmers in behalf of the international community. Core and periphery issues would not improve for nations with limited natural resources. Contrary to popular belief, legalization will invite transnational corporations to control a business that has been largely saved as a family controlled economic system. A perfect example is the competition created among marihuana entrepreneur bars in California. Organized franchises have emerged and slowly have been controlling a free enterprise system many believed would open the doors to the "get rich quick" dream driven by the process to legalize drugs.

Societal development under a legalized drug system, for the agrarian cultures, would pursue the usual capitalist adventures characteristics of core versus periphery economies. The lifestyle for the farmers would probably suffer a decline against the technical advances used to generate large crops for global distribution. The "banana republic" controls by selected few may continue its controls by the same elitist groups. Legal maneuvers could network against the poor and middle class currently engaged in illegal production, processing, and international distribution. The new breed of rising wealthy men, so eager to maneuver their clandestine profits into acceptable social recognition, may instead suffer a decrease in personal income.

Once the legalized production increases, the cast of middlemen responsible for illegal trading among the Andean communities could be eliminated in behalf of Wall Street style businessmen responsible for absolute control over the most profitable crops at a worldwide level. College educated professionals will take over the transnational trading, creating a more competitive market that aims at price increases to meet the needs of the international legalized network. The middlemen opportunities to create a fortune that is challenged with the money laundering process will become casualties in exchange for the Wall Street college educated professionals. The illegal infrastructure capable of lavish income for formerly poor and disadvantaged under a subterranean economy will become another casualty of the legalization process.

Illegal laboratories established for the underground refinement of coca leaves into crack cocaine will also suffer at the hands of international pharmaceutical companies. It is unlikely countries like the United States of America will legalize drugs and allow small businessmen to process and determine the quantities, chemicals, additives, and all the laboratory process. The Food and Drug Administration (FDA) will have to determine acceptable standards, and the drug status of these crops will undergo serious scrutiny to make sure the production levels of crack and cocaine are under the control of reliable and reputable corporations that specialize in that field to meet medical standards. This brings another issue that will adversely affect the benefits received by small illegal entrepreneurs.

The small business production of illegal drugs such as cocaine will suffer a great loss under a legalized drug system. Underground illegal laboratories will be considered substandard in comparison to recognized pharmaceutical corporations. The manpower used by the cartels and middlemen to produce the illegal products in underground laboratories would also lose credibility and its sustainability would be eliminated. Sterile production conditions would be required by the FDA and production control would fall under major laboratories around the world. It is reasonable to assume growers may have to meet inspection, similar to the standards under the US Department of Agriculture (USDAG), and receive an acceptable grade based on a government designed scale to rate the production quality. A similar process used on tobacco growers will have to be implemented, measuring different substance levels of chemicals and substances used during the planting, growing, and harvesting process. The measure will likely force small farmers out of business in a domino effect that will decrease production, increase prices, and continue to prevent small farmer competition in behalf of larger international enterprises. Government controls will likely force an increase in prices. Recent efforts by the AFL-CIO to unionize the marijuana farmers and workers in California will also bring demands and controls likely to result in increased prices. Business as usual, importing the raw material cheaper from across the border under NAFTA may also create an outcry from the American pot farmers.

Global competition to purchase the raw material would again become a factor in a large price increase per ton, the measure gauge used to sell coca leaf. The domino effect would trigger the market competition of chemical companies that continue to profit from diversifying chemicals for the production of coca paste. Legalization would create competitive markets, which would also cut down on the exorbitant profit margin levels generated by front corporations that funnel the needed chemicals from producing agents. The identification of these chemicals would, in turn, create adverse reactions against the use of acetone and potassium chloride in favor of less harmful chemicals used in cocaine paste production. This would add to the continuum effect that will adversely affect the profit margins and actors involved in illegal drug trade. Exchanging less harmful chemicals will require extensive laboratory testing, which will result in the typical transfer of expenses to the consumer. Your typical rock will cost a lot more to offset the expenses of PhD's, medical technicians, calibrating tools, and fancy sterile labs.

The US Government (USG) will be forced to establish guidelines on the type of chemicals used in the production of cocaine. Laboratory testing will be required to determine alternative safe chemical agents needed to achieve the same effect created by these market drugs. Before reaching that step, a control at the global level must be established to dictate the type of chemicals used as fertilizers and pesticides at the agricultural level. Tobacco production, for example, has been targeted by the FDA for years to dictate acceptable nicotine levels. The health effects caused by cigarettes prompted massive action from government agencies, and an outcry from the population that netted lawyers a steady financial security for decades. The "sin" tax is always applied to tobacco and alcohol consumers, driving the prices upward without any future relief. This is part of the certain future of legalization. "Turf wars" between different cartels and dealers will become a fad of the past under a government controlled system. However, once the government becomes your drug dealer, a sleuth of measures will have an adverse and positive effect on the "law abiding" citizens.

The transportation of the raw material will have to meet specific guidelines, in addition to any additives utilized to preserve its freshness, when taking the raw material from South America into laboratories in the USA, Europe, Russia, the Middle East, or wherever purchased. It is possible to establish transnational pharmaceutical corporations in the countries blessed with these natural resources, depriving the continental USA from generating needed income. Once the raw material enters the USA, the pharmaceutical corporations will be under the obligation to engage in costly research studies to convert cocaine into a less noxious product. Testing required for the elimination of harsh chemicals such as acetone and potassium chloride from the processing level, or the reduction of percentages, such as claims of what has been done with the use of coke syrup in the manufacture of Coca-Cola, will undoubtedly be passed as an expense to the addicted public segment. The chemical diversifying industry profits from the illegal processing of raw material into cocaine will likely decline once the legalization process demands action from the FDA.

A quick search on the chemicals used to process coca leaves into cocaine hydrochloride (1) reinforces why it is unlikely that chemicals such as cocaine will be included as legalized drugs. The process begins with the need to identify two out of seventeen species of coca leaves that contain the highest levels of alkaloids needed to create paste and hydrochloric alkaloids. The chemicals used in the process make everyone wonder on why anyone in their right mind would select to use crack-cocaine or any of its derivatives for human consumption. Among the basic stages one finds the use of kerosene fuel to separate the right ingredients, followed by sodium carbonate, which does not create concern if used in small dosages. The following stages follow with the uses of sulfuric acid, hydrochloric acid, and potassium permanganate. If you believe these are not worrisome enough, they need to add ammonia and acetone (or ether) to finalize the production into its marketing base.

Public recognition of the use of these ingredients in processing a legalized drug will create an outcry to research and modify the chemicals used to provide the addicted public with an acceptable drug endorsed by the FDA. This will definitely have an impact on the core businesses responsible for diversifying the products sale for the benefit of illegal drug producers. In addition, it will be mandatory to test other chemicals in an effort to supply a better product. How likely is it for the FDA to approve a product in which gasoline, acetone, ether and potassium chloride are ingested in one way or another? The quality seeds needed to obtain plants capable of producing good quality coca paste will have to be purchased from either Peru or Bolivia. Qualified laboratory personnel will be needed to determine the botanical species required to produce quality paste base. The coca leaf produced in Colombia, for example, is of lower quality than the ones produced in Peru and Bolivia. Growing these plants will require certain environmental controls that promote growth. Most of the species grow in altitude areas between 1,900 and 6,000 feet above sea level. Temperature levels, humidity controls, and the ability to control fungus and diseases are challenges to be met that could be solved by pharmaceutical companies. Purchase of the varieties needed to produce good quality products will not be an easy task if our intention is to create competition with developing nations.

Although the political system component in this agenda has not been addressed in this segment, the American public has the largest appetite for crack-cocaine than any other world population. The process of "Bolivarización" has demonstrated, so far, a hostile psychology against the United States of America. Many South American and Central American countries have criticized democracy and capitalism as evil in the establishment process of Bolivarization. Taking that animosity into consideration may result in accepting that the American public may become a financial target if the Latin American producing nations refuse to sell the raw product to American laboratories. The same petroleum blackmail played by Hugo Chavez could be exercised by the coca producing nations. Innovative entrepreneurship will probably drive American investors to design massive greenhouses to grow coca leaves. Regardless of whether we decide to legalize drugs or not, we must begin the preparation stages to accept as global exchange the "virtual currency," which has become an issue of transnational dialogue within the new league of Latin American nations. Repeated requests to pay for Venezuelan oil with Eurodollars may be extended to other raw materials. We could speculate on a price increase for coca if demands force us to pay for the raw material with Eurodollars, or a "virtual currency," instead of American dollars.

So far, we have been able to see how legalization will create a domino effect that begins with the small farmer and the raw material, and engages the middle man. The drug kingpin and cartel networks, under a legalized drug distribution system, will be expected to collapse after losing their business infrastructure. It is unlikely that these figures will utilize their wealth and profits to meet commercial standards. It is almost impossible to assume they will vanish into omission feeling satisfied that their successful efforts forced the legalization of drugs. More than likely, the cartels, as institutions, will expect a certain level of integration into the marketing strata in gratitude for nearly a century worth of sweat, as well as blood spilled through violent turf wars. Kingpin survivors must also be recognized as the driving force behind the legalization process. At some point, we may even read books written by these most educated criminals, or their heritage line, on the myriad of American politicians and businesses responsible for the failures in national policies aimed at deterring the destruction of American youth. This would make them a threat to the *de juro* politicians and businessmen responsible for the deterrents encountered by law enforcement agencies during the war on drugs. These are the individuals that have maintained these drugs at an illegal level.

The diversification process used by the cartels and underworld figures indicate that it is unlikely their integration into the legal drug business will become reality. A brief historical comparison with the "Roaring Twenties" may serve as a brief reminder that a violent outburst responsible for the deaths of many bootleggers was the rule of law. If we compare the magnitude of the alcohol prohibition years with the transnational complexities involved in the illegal drug business, we could convince the kingpins and cartels on how much safer their business deals are in the "pre-legalization" era. It could almost convince them that political actors involved in the illegal drug dealings and business would feel inclined to eliminate any evidence, actors, and their off springs from shattering their decades of contributions to the physical and mental decay of America's society. Furthermore, we may even be able to introduce the idea that narco-terrorist groups would reap financial benefits from the elimination of the cartel infrastructure. The political, socio-economic mesh supporting drug traffic today may shatter at the hands of narco-terrorist groups responsible for financing their activities through drug cartels. We have revisited this issue in another chapter, but it is a key part of the cartel benefits while drugs are illegal.

Preservation of the cartel's infrastructure financial status is possible through "drug bootlegging," which is likely to surface after drugs are legalized. It is highly unlikely that the governments will legalize drugs where each individual will have the freedom and liberty to purchase drugs as often as they want. Legalizing alcohol was a taxation process over sold goods where obviously the effects over individuals and their family or social impact was secondary and irrelevant. The ridiculous expectation that government will only legalize what is beneficial to the population serves as a humble reminder that most governments fail the test of their intentions for the constituents in exchange for power and personal wealth. Government restrictions will be created that will probably include a quota available for drug purchase, mirrored on initiatives established in other countries.

Emerging patterns in cities involved in legalization indicate that once an individual consumes their allowed quantities, they will probably be required to engage on some level of drug rehabilitation process. A consumer's registry, in this case, must be generated to provide the names of individuals entitled to consume prescribed illegal drugs. Once an individual uses all their refills, they will automatically receive notification of their need to engage in rehabilitation treatment. Such individuals will have two options: receive treatment or opt out. An individual engaged in the rehabilitative process, which will likely be paid under some type of federal and/or state drug rehabilitation fund, will have a record on file which identifies the individual wherever it goes. Addicts that opt out will likely pay other addicts to obtain prescriptions or drugs, instead of complying with the government source. Their other resource will probably be the street dealers still available to supply illegal drugs, or the emerging trendy "drug bootlegger." "Drug bootleggers" will likely charge exorbitant prices to compensate for the financial losses created by legalization.

Benefits for drug addicts must be available by the government in different areas. First, the concept of "international health care reform" must be implemented at a global level to meet the needs of all the drug addicts entitled to their "fix" under government subsidy. Indigent dependents on the welfare system must be able to hold a card or identification to obtain free drugs, the same way we identify Medicaid patients. We must prepare to meet the needs of "drug addict tourists," as countries with legalized drugs have met an upsurge of visitors from other countries. A dilemma will ensue on the availability of drugs for citizens versus visiting tourists; which may multiply when American taxpayers face the prospect of drug benefits available for illegal immigrants.

Our focus remains on the adverse effects suffered by a drug addict when they are diagnosed and labeled as suffering from the illness of drug addiction. Emerging trends in the area apparently provide social justifications for those suffering from the illness of addiction, in a similar fashion as those suffering from atherosclerosis, diabetes, strokes, epilepsy, and the never-ending list of diseases. Although the current trend to prescribe marihuana as legalized medicine is beginning to increase, we have yet begun to see government action to curtail the "organic" home grower's attempts to establish their nurseries and garden centers. The differentiation between the uses of marihuana versus the use of crack-cocaine products imposes a standard that will be met by society against the legalization of crack cocaine products. Legalization of drugs currently unavailable due to federal restrictions will still suffer discriminative practices due to adverse primary and secondary effects. This issue is very important when we take into consideration the fact that most crack-cocaine addicts began their addiction using marihuana. In addition, federal failure to accept crack-cocaine as a legal drug may continue the perpetual problematic associated to illegal drug trade.

Stepping back to the measures available to control drug addiction in our country leads us to establish standards and measures available to provide medical services to those suffering from medicinal addiction. Once a person's record includes medical drug addiction, it will be our social responsibility to provide measures that maintain such individuals as productive members of society. The medical records, however, will be available to employers to impose the responsibility levels required from such individual. This availability may hinder opportunities to obtain employment if the records are available. Current health care reform openly stipulates that medical records will be available, under the current proposals, to be carried over from one employer to the next without any discrimination. Productivity levels from such individuals could be easily detected based on additional healthcare visits required under the law, detoxification treatment, and hospital or institution internment. This is the worst case scenario to be suffered for legalization of harsh drugs such as crack-cocaine, which in 2010 is very unlikely to happen.

Since the likelihood of legalizing crack-cocaine and its derivatives is very limited, we must look at which segment of cocaine would be likely to appeal to the American public. Peruvian and Bolivian indigenous forces chew fresh coca leaves during rituals and drink its tea form to cure ailments and maladies. Legalization of these two forms is likely to appeal to the American public for daily consumption, avoiding the ingestion and exposure to the list of harmful chemicals used in coca products. The claim that Coca-Cola Company is still allowed to use minute levels of coca in its products indicates our government is likely to accept some percent of this substance. This drives us to investigate, on the other hand, the acceptance in certain states to use marihuana for "medicinal" purpose, and how the government is likely to allow "free enterprise" identification before engaging in the most massive government intrusion in the American homes before "federal" drug legalization takes place. Keep in mind that the purpose of this section is to recognize if illegal drug users and producers will really benefit from legalization.

LEGALIZING MARIHUANA

Legalization of marihuana for medicinal purposes is the initial stage introduced to force a medical control roster of those addicted to marihuana use. Doctors, clinics, and patients are required to disclose any information about their patient's drug use if the patient changes doctors. The law in California (2) also states that prescription can be provided by any physician, but the physician is responsible for evaluating the patient long enough to determine if marihuana will be prescribed. Records must be transferred to a new assigned physician, if the patient changes doctors, although it is the patient's responsibility to provide required information to the new doctor. The accepted standards to recommend marihuana prescriptions include at this time, and I quote:

- "History and good faith examination of the patient."
- "Development of a treatment plan with objectives."
- "Provision of informed consent including discussion of side effects."
- "Periodic review of the treatment's efficacy."
- "Consultation, as necessary."
- "Also, proper record keeping that supports the decision to recommend the use of medical marijuana."

The recommendation follows through with the following statement, which creates liability not necessarily with the patient, but with its family and federal law enforcement officials:

"… if physicians use the same care in recommending medical marijuana to patients as they would recommending or approving any other medication, they have nothing to fear from the Medical Board."

Other points taken into consideration in California when recommending medical marijuana:

1. "Although it could trigger federal action, making a recommendation in writing to the patient will not trigger action by the Medical Board of California."
2. "A patient need not have failed on all standard medications, in order for a physician to recommend or approve the use of medical marijuana."

Initially, the use of medicinal marihuana was based on its natural medicinal value, but item number 2 indicates that there is actually no established standard to prescribe the use of marihuana as any other prescribed drug. Use of marihuana as a medicine in California is no longer based on the failure of obtaining relief using other legal prescription drugs. The following items also indicate that, although marihuana was introduced as a cure under the "The Compassionate Use Act of 1996," the current decision for prescribing it as a drug falls under any medical condition category. Neither critical illness nor conditions in which patients are under excruciating pain are taken into consideration to determine the need to use this otherwise recreational drug, based on the following passage:

3. "The Act names certain medical conditions for which medical marijuana may be useful, although physicians are not limited in their recommendations to those specific conditions. In all cases, the physician should base his/her determination on the results of clinical trials, if available, medical literature and reports, or on experience of that physician or other physicians, or on credible patient reports. In all cases, **the** physician must determine that the risk/benefit ratio of medical marijuana is as good, or better, than other medications that could be used for that individual patient."
4. "An initial visit by the patient is still recommended, but not required…" which lends itself to misrepresentation costly under the many cases of identity theft. Removing marihuana medical consumption from one's personal medical record may create a nightmare situation for law abiding citizens concerned with their reputation as abiding by the law.
5. "The initial examination for the condition for which medical marijuana is being recommended must be in-person."

6. "Recommendations should be limited to the time necessary to appropriately monitor the patient. Periodic reviews should occur and be documented at least annually or more frequently as warranted."
7. "If a physician recommends or approves the use of medical marijuana for a minor, the parents or legal guardians must be fully informed of the risks and benefits of such use and must consent to that use."

Physicians may wish to refer to CMA's ON-CALL Document #1315 titled "The Compassionate Use Act of 1996," (3) updated annually for additional information and guidance. Although the Compassionate Use Act allows the use of medical marijuana by a patient upon the recommendation or approval of a physician, California physicians should bear in mind that is listed in Schedule I of the federal Controlled Substances Act, which means that it has no accepted medical use under federal law. However, in Conant v. Walters (9th Cir.2002) F.3d 629 the United States Court of Appeals recognized that physicians have a constitutionally-protected right to discuss medical marijuana as a treatment option with their patients and make oral or written recommendation for its use. The court cautioned that physicians could exceed the scope of this constitutional protection if they "... conspire with, or aid and abet their patients in obtaining medical marijuana."

In other words, the government in California has overstepped its authority in violation of federal law. The State of California has legalized the use of marihuana yet, instead of supporting the prescribing doctors and users, it clearly states that they will be responsible for defending their decisions in federal court. It is also making clear that a continuous patient-doctor relationship must exist during the duration of the "therapy" process. This supports the initial stage required to force patients into a state or federal roster that identifies individuals using what is still an illegal drug under federal mandates. The next step is being circumvented by the new wave of entrepreneurs offering advice on how to grow the crop, or opening "drug cafes" that facilitate illegal drugs.

Law abiding citizens and the federal government are entitled to several steps to support these business enterprises willing to provide expertise on self-medication and engaging on production of medication to protect patients from tampering that may cause potential damage. Let's look at how the cafes and "Pot Home-growers," or PHg's, must be accountable under the law. Educators are required by law to become state or national certified as knowledgeable on the subject matter they teach. Anyone engaged in teaching agriculture must be state certified as a qualified instructor or teacher. Legal establishments teaching how to produce marihuana, or selling the seeds or "starter sets," must be accountable for their expertise to be able to dispense knowledge on the production, processing, sterile conditions, and sale of a government controlled substance. An agency responsible for such certification and licensure must be recognized first at a federal level, such as the Drug Enforcement Administration, since they are experts in the subject matter of drugs.

Failure to empower the DEA to provide such certification, since their expertise is in law enforcement and not on administration of drug production, will undoubtedly shift required certification under the FDA. This creates a rather compromising and challenging situation. Since marihuana is considered a controlled substance, dispensing marihuana, as well as providing expertise on the production and consumption process of this drug will eventually require the same federal requirements as Lipitor, Penicillin, and other medication prescribed by doctors. FDA requires production of medicines under laboratory control, where doctors and medical technicians create drugs under **sterile** conditions.

A conflict of interest arises when some prescribed drugs are produced under sterile conditions, if others can be produced at home. Accountability from the PHg's and home-growers is desirable to ensure they will not become "expert" doctors on the field without the appropriate education and credentials. Research on how to grow coca leaf helped us understand that there are different varieties of coca capable of producing different levels of alkaloids. Although not an expert on marihuana growth, it is clear that there are several varieties to be grown, with benefits that include higher or lower potency. Benefits to our population should require from the FDA some research and investigation as to which marihuana plants are better to provide the relief level sought by doctors and patients. The variety used on adults, for example, should not be the same dosage prescribed to children under the age of six. Laboratory tests must provide accurate disclosure of the grams required per marihuana species to reach the effective medical level, similar to the requirements for all other prescription drugs.

There is no statistical evidence we could find of research conducted on the potency of marijuana prior to the "hippie" generation. Since then, beginning in the 1980's, research conducted indicated the potency level was as high as a level four (4). Recent disclosures from government agencies indicate the tetrahydrocannabinol (THC) levels on tested species has raised to a potency level 11, almost triple the THC levels found in the

1980's. This becomes a serious issue that must be addressed by the FDA, because doctors are prescribing it as a medication to adults AND children. The lack of regulation on the potency of this "medicine" prescribed to kids and adults of all ages in an indiscriminately form, may cause an overdose and/or serious side effects.

This issue is of special concern if these children will be attending school systems under the influence of prescriptions that are not scientifically adjusted to the personal needs of each individual. The school systems, under the "No Child Left Behind" law, would have to provide special accommodations due to their medical condition. Further more, the parents of these children must inform the school systems in California that their children are using a mood altering drug. A complication in this case is the fact that federal assistance to students under the influence of illegal drugs requires the schools to seek assistance for the students for drug addiction. Students applying for federal assistance to attend college are not allowed to use controlled substances under federal law. This almost creates a judicial liability at the federal level for child abuse and neglect against the licensed doctors involved. It also creates a double standard against the states refusing to legalize marijuana.

A prescription by a licensed doctor is given to a patient after taking into consideration several factors that need to be improved. The correct brand is a factor, along with the grams or potency required to correct the malady or disease. Both of these factors adversely affect children, since there is actually no regulation or regulators capable of scientific disclosure of these components. Failure to disclose the THC level, as well as proving the marijuana served in the café, grown at home, or purchased in the streets, has been scientifically tested could result in children consuming the inappropriate dosage. This may lead to a drug addiction level beyond and above the child's healthcare needs. Worst, it may lead to a doctor approved creation of young addicts, especially if the child's condition is not death threatening. This indicator, again, points at the need to have the FDA regulate the research, production and distribution of marijuana prescribed by licensed doctors and physicians. This also proves there is a need for patients to have the ability to purchase this type of medication from a reputable source. Failure to purchase the medication from a reputable source still lends itself to the risk of purchasing laced products with other highly addictive or harmful herbs and chemicals.

Medicines like Sativex and Marinol are produced with extracts, but are considered very expensive in comparison to the street value paid for a joint. The side effects of laboratory produced medication may inhibit consumers and create a preference for the natural product. Marijuana use causes tobacco-like side effects such as lung cancer with an equivalent ratio of five (5) joints versus a pack of 20 cigarettes. It is also linked to lung and airway diseases due to the smoke. The side effects created to tissue also generate immune system deficiencies that become harder to control. Side effects, therefore, are easily eliminated as an excuse to use the street products. The FDA could also claim production in pharmaceutical controlled laboratories would meet the appropriate needs of consumers at all age levels. This will lead to a government controlled enterprise that would still be able to preserve the usefulness of government agencies like the DEA and local anti-narcotic units.

The decision to legalize medical use of marihuana has unleashed a wave of marihuana growers, entrepreneurs, and "how-to-grow" professors without a license. Recent remarks in 2009 from the President of the United States of America, Barack Hussein Obama, specified the DEA must focus its efforts on enforcing the law against higher echelons in the drug war, and leave the addict users alone. Based on this premise, how will drug cafes and marihuana selling establishments rate, since they are not actually patients but dealers and producers of an illegal substance? Will these entrepreneurs be considered drug dealers, or just average businessmen? Should patients be considered experts in the subject matter because they consume, or maybe grow THC products? A double standard in this case may send a conflicting message to other drug dealers and consumers, reinforcing the need to revisit whether all drugs should be legalized. If they are legalized, then we need to look again, as in the case of legalizing crack-cocaine, at how we will be able to enforce legalization without disrupting social standards, principles, and moral behavior.

It is necessary to investigate how we will be able to deal with legalizing marihuana on a step by step basis. The city of Bogota, Colombia, legalized the use of drugs but failed to establish standards for consumption. This generated a revision, first on how much drug would a citizen be able to consume or hold in its possession. Translation: drug possession is still punishable by law if you exceed your quota. Another issue became obvious when citizens began to use their "bazuco" (lower quality of cocaine product) in public, in front of adults as well as children. The government added to existing laws the need to consume legalized levels of drugs in the privacy of their home and away from children. Unlike California, the Colombian lawmakers still believe children are not entitled to consume controlled substances. At a time when schools have passed laws banning tobacco products, one could question the reasons behind permitting students to enter a school while under the influence of drugs, even if it is legalized marijuana. Legalization requires a lot of research in several areas, and there are many questions that need to be answered to prevent major problems faced by countries that considered legalization as the best remedy to the losses suffered during the "war on drugs."

The advantages and disadvantages of dispensing drugs through licensed physicians is important to make sure patients have a medical need before they are allowed to purchase and consume drugs like marijuana. This means that the masses of people roaming street corners purchasing marijuana will not be entitled to purchase drugs because they lack a disease or medical condition that merits medication. The moral dilemma begins immediately, as the whole purpose of legalizing marijuana, the most benign of herbs you can smoke according to some, is to solve the illegal drug problem. The medicinal use of marijuana could be extended to regular addicts IF they agree to recognize their addiction as a medical problem under mental health care. This begins to differentiate the medical needs of some based on a physical and psychological condition, versus psychological and mental problems in others.

The same requirements forced on patients that must maintain "contact" with their medical professional, will be required of the addicts that suffer from "mental/emotional" conditions. These other patients will have to maintain "contact" with their mental health provider to be able to purchase their THC medication. Most prescription drugs stipulate a quantity available for purchase, a given timeline, and "X" amount of refills before visiting their physician. These controls require a visit to the physician in most cases. Everyone, regardless of their socio-economic level, will be identified as a THC drug user. Under a legalized system, everyone will be required to visit a physician for prescriptions, usually dispensed by approved and certified pharmacies. This also brings the issue of production.

The street value of marijuana is fairly reasonable because it is produced anywhere, and sold everywhere. FDA approved drugs must meet specific standards usually produced in controlled environments. In April 2009 the House of Representatives introduced HR 2134 IH, a little advertised bill called the **Western Hemisphere Drug Policy Commission Act of 2009.** (4) This 10-member commission is empowered to:

"...review and evaluate United States illicit drug supply policy, with particular emphasis on international drug policies and programs directed toward the countries of the Western Hemisphere and demand reduction policies and programs. The Commission would identify policy and program options to improve existing international and domestic counternarcotics policy."

The commission will create federal options and policies to override existing counternarcotics policies. Word from insiders indicates this is the first step from the federal government to justify legalization of street drugs in the USA. The USAG is taking into consideration many factors, which include medical and mental health care, crime control, and financial benefits. Recent economic global collapse was saved, according to some economy experts, by the subterranean economic infrastructure created by illegal drug money. So, one may assume that our Congressional elected officials may be interested in an equal distribution of this cash generated by this *de facto* economic system. In this case, it will be extremely possible for the United States of America to legalize drugs, at least some types. After all, the end of the Prohibition Era brought the government's ability to tax prohibited goods and became a fair share holder of the profits. Nearly a century later we recognize legalizing alcohol did not solve the problem, but the fact that Congress legalized it led people to believe if it was legal it must not have been bad for people.

This point is addressed because of the financial issues legalization will generate, which will adversely affect consumers of what we know today as illegal drugs. Production of drugs will require a sterile environment. Street vendors, THC-Cafes, cooperative groups, THC Colleges, and all the self-made entrepreneurs are likely to suffer economic collapse under the legalization process. The usual first beneficiaries from government initiatives are selected groups, in this case pharmaceutical companies. Drugs must be produced in sterile, controlled environments where research and testing meets specific guidelines. The second winners in the legalization process will be the health insurance companies' ability to increase premiums based on a target population with an appetite for drugs that includes two thirds of the world consumption. The USA government will be the third winner for diverting a global market profit into the USA's economy.

Incredible as it may seem, there are many losers in legalization, and they are, mostly, the naïve individuals that believed the best option to the war on drugs was legalization. First losers will be the addicts that could purchase drugs "freely" in the streets. These individuals will pay a very high price for herbs produced in sterile environments controlled by high paid technicians in white robes. They will pay for the researcher's expertise, the production in controlled environments, and distribution of goods processed through private companies, such as pharmaceuticals which are known for driving the prices of medication to sky-high levels. They will be subject to availability controls enforced through their doctors, counselors, and pharmacies. They will also have to pay a physician that must certify the individual suffers from a medical or mental condition. They will be subject to a physician's determination on the quantity and quality of drugs available for consumption. They will also have a government controlled record of chemical dependency available for federal and state scrutiny. Part of the legalization process in other countries includes the required therapy sessions and detoxification process required once individuals reach their consumption quota. Therefore, the medical records will serve as a control to determine which individuals are addicted to the former illegal drugs. Benefits to society will include providing needed therapy for these individuals, which under a "war on drugs" would be anonymous undetectable figures that blend in a multitude of statistical reports. The statistics under a legalized drug dependency will have a name and address traceable for enforcement.

Under optimal conditions, effective detoxification programs will be available to provide better alternatives to addiction. Similar to Alcoholics Anonymous, methadone treatment, and other substitutes may eventually replace THC with laboratory designed drugs. During this process, federal and state mandated healthcare system will be made available as part of our national health care proposal in 2010. In exchange for legalized drugs, addicted individuals will probably be committed to state-run care or institutions capable of providing drug rehabilitation services. A revolving door system will ensue, which will probably make addicts wish they had never considered legalization. Drug addicts, however, could circumvent the process and begin a new "bootlegging" system, paying other individuals for their personal prescriptions at a higher price level. This will eventually lead to a creation and support of the black market system, and begin the recycling door process again.

The "entrepreneur" level of THC Café's, dispensaries, and cannabis clubs will disappear, or may become part of the bureaucratic taxation process imposed on small businesses and franchises. It is amazing these businesses have not been required to pay for a specific license operating under state controlled guidelines. In addition, it is even more amazing that these establishments have not been rated with an inspection passing level on a scale of 70% to 100%, requiring a lower level to close their doors or comply with government mandated quality. The self-appointed expert instructors of "Cannabis Colleges" and "how-to-grow-pot" gurus will probably have to diversify their expertise into a new business venture capable of providing "potting pot kits" available at your nearest medicinal landscape nursery. The same will probably happen to food producers that lace products with controlled substances. FDA will probably step demands to identify ingredients used in preparation anytime drugs are used to lace edible products. Again, compliance with federal and state laws may result in one of several controls.

Accurate purchase record of any cannabis product or base plant must be required with a drug prescription, with limits based on federally established guidelines. Failure to request appropriate identification will result in (additional taxation) fines up to $200,000 due to pharmaceutical prescription violations. Once licenses and certificates become a requirement for operations, the loss of a license will become another issue to contend with to maintain a business open. Preservation of the Drug Enforcement Agency will be possible due to their capacity to enforce federal drug laws, so law enforcement agencies will exist even if legalization is established. It is a fact that cities that have legalized drugs have not extended the legalization process to all drugs available in the black market.

A legal process to engage in the sale, distribution, and facilitation of the controlled substance will have to be established to preserve legal guarantees. It is obvious that, taking these issues in consideration, HR 2134 IH aims at generating billions of dollars at the national level that have been siphoned out of the economy for decades. The disturbing component of the bill, however, will ignore the fact that drug addiction induces a low level of performance on the consumers. Restrictions forced on tobacco growers will have to be imposed in a similar manner on growers. It is very unlikely to assume that our pharmaceutical companies will have the facilities to produce large quantities of laboratory controlled marijuana. It is also unlikely that the will be available in a carton, like cigarettes. More than likely, it will be available in a "six-pack" box, still sold at your nearest pharmacy. "Bootlegging" and illegal drug sales will still be an issue, diverting economic resources to a fewer selection of businessmen. The cost of illegal drugs after legalization will be much higher. Addicts, and proponents of legalization, must take these issues into consideration before biting into the bait of legal access.

Congressional proposals to study the impact of legalization have also looked at other issues related to illegal drug trade. In addition to the concerns established, the new trends in Washington, DC assume our majority population is ready for the next step. The networks linked to illegal drug trade may be the actual reason why our congressmen are adventurous in leading the process. The following chapters may actually provide a better picture on the reasons why the American public may want to engage in reviewing the pros and cons of legalizing drugs, or may decide to seek healthcare to avoid drug addiction. The subject area that has not taken public review is called the process of Bolivarization. The main reason why legalization of drugs in the USA is related to the subject of *bolivarizacion,* or Bolivarization, is due to the connection established with an underground transnational network. The funneling of funding from illegal drug sales into the arms race and the terrorist groups will suffer a great impact. Illegal drug trade has proven to be the most transforming and versatile enterprise throughout decades. It is possible to assume, therefore, that the crack-cocaine illegal drug trade will survive since there are more behavior aberrations associated to coca and its derivatives. This will provide the economic source to the emerging network of narco-guerrilla terrorist groups settling in the Western Hemisphere. Decades of attempts to destroy the superpower status of the United States of America have proven to be unsuccessful, even with terrorist attacks.

Historically, superpower nations self-destroy with overindulgence and their uncanny appetite to satisfy the "me, myself, and I." Almost a decade after the September 11, 2001 attacks, we have experienced a decline in illegal drug consumption even with a rise in production in Afghanistan and the poppy producing nations. Within the same time period, thirteen states in the USA have legalized marihuana for medicinal purposes, bringing the total of those that have legalized it, and those with proposals to legalize it to twenty five states. The House of Representatives has begun its study on the benefits of legalizing drugs. Taken into consideration the diverse methodology applied to enact health care reform, it is clear the same Congress has the potential to pass legislation to legalize drugs in the USA.

Nations around the world have joined efforts among our enemies to force a decline in the American society. American citizens, on the average, do not suffer from what will be labeled a dependency on drugs, and have been distant on initiatives from the federal and state governments to control the illegal drug problematic. Reading news of young people in Latin America forced into addiction by guerrilla groups is heartbreaking. Knowing that the drug addiction epidemic in the USA has been created by dealers to enrich the drug trafficking network is outrageous. A discredit to our society will surface if Americans allow our younger generations to become addicted through programs subsidized by our own government because it will prove claims that the USA government has been the power wheel behind the illegal drug network. Passing legislation in Washington DC to legalize drugs will probably imply that the economic disaster forced upon the American public will run aligned with contributing to the self-destruction of the United States of America.

End Notes:

(1) "Coca Cultivation and Cocaine Processing." **Marihuana Business News.com**. Retrieved from: http://www.druglibrary.org/schaffer/GovPubs/COCCCP.htm.

(2) The Compassionate Use Act of 1996. **The Medical Board of California**. Retrieved from: http://www.medbd.ca.gov/medical_.html

(3) CMA's ON-CALL Document #1315 titled "The Compassionate Use Act of 1996." Retrieved from http://www.cmanet.org/bookstore/freeoncall2.cfm/CMAOnCall1315.pdf?call_nu mber=1315&CFID=745764&CFTOKEN=27566287

(4) Western Hemisphere Drug Policy Commission Act of 2009. Retrieved from www.gop.gov/bill/111/1/hr2134.

Johansmeyer, Tom. (2009, Nov 15). "First US café opens for business in Portland." Retrieved from http://www.dailyfinance.com/2009/11/15/first-u-s--cafe-opens-for-business-in-portland.

CHAPTER II

"BOLIVARIZACION"
The Historical Background Of "Bolivarization:"

Will the USA Congressional bill study the Bolivarization process before deciding in favor or against legalizing drugs?

Rituals and traditions in the South American Andean region include the use of coca leaves, a practice that has never been condemned by the United States of America Government (USAG). The history of the Andean region also demonstrates the Spaniards encouraged the indigenous tribes to chew coca leaves. Chewing coca leaves quenched hunger pains and deprived the Andean natives from recognizing they were enslaved to long hours of hard labor. The first step leading to the conclusion of whether addicts want the legalization of controlled substances is a brief account of the historical movements that have nurtured the global marketing of illegal drugs. The readers seeking to legalize controlled drugs must base their decision on an educated choice, which must begin with the original politics that have led to international relations, global economies, the creation of Drug Enforcement Agencies and the Food and Drug Administration. Your patience walking through the different steps is the only key available to support an intelligent and rational decision capable of changing current laws.

Latin America suffered enslavement from the Spanish and Portuguese conquerors, which eventually led to the movements leading to independence in the region. The natives in the Andean region utilized the coca leaves in several ways. They chewed the leaves to prevent and soothe the pains created by high altitude, as the coca leaves contain a chemical that constricts the blood vessels. The medicinal values of the coca *mate*, a tea brew, have also received recognition. Incan descendants used the coca leaves during rituals that nurtured bonding within the tribe, which has led to the quasi acceptance that within the indigenous cultures the use of coca leaves is an acceptable practice that contributes to the cultural development in the region.

The worst scenario created by the Spaniards in the Andean region was the use of the traditional rituals using coca leaves. Coca leave is the raw material needed to produce cocaine and its derivatives, and it must not be alternated nor confused as the modern source of illegal drug trade. However, the Spaniards were able to recognize the values associated to the rituals, and the benefits reaped by allowing the Incan descendants to chew coca leaves. Allowing the indigenous slaves to chew coca leaves desensitized the native's ability to perceive when they were hungry, thirsty, or tired. Hard labor in the mines and servitude to the conquerors became extremely profitable in two flanks: the indigenous force worked from sunrise to sunset without realizing they had been enslaved; plus, their healthcare and well-being was unrecognizable due to the coca side effects. The side effects prevented them from taking care of themselves due to their failure to recognize when they were sick, tired, and in need of medication or treatment to restore their health. Coca leaves, in essence, enabled the Spaniards to institutionalize one of the first cases of forced hard labor by medicating an occupied region.

Latin American studies have recognized the contributions of Simon Bolivar and the wars of independence throughout South America. Bolivar has been identified throughout the Western Hemisphere, as well as Europe, as the catalyst force responsible for the successful movement removing the Spaniards as an occupying force in South America. It is almost possible to state that his actions, inspired by the independence movements in the United States of America and European models, led the rest of Latin America to seek independence from the Europeans. Even Karl Marx acknowledged Bolivar as a crucial actor involved in the fights for freedom in the Western Hemisphere. Directly or indirectly he had an impact in either supporting or encouraging the liberation movements in many South American nations. The treatment received by the natives during the early colonial centuries, as well as the treatment suffered by African slaves brought by the European settlers, was in need of correction. Regardless of the movements to abolish slavery, which were initiated in part by the

Catholic Church, the damage served as a catalyst to precipitate a movement that, amazingly, remained in incubation for nearly two centuries.

The term "bolivarización" (bolivarization) has been reintroduced after almost a century and a half of exposure to the term. Hugo Chavez in Venezuela has spoken about his "right" to reintroduce bolivarization because he claims to be the "reincarnation" of Simon Bolivar. It could be a humorous statement, taking into consideration this is the same president that claims the United States has been testing an earthquake producing weapon in Haiti, after a major earthquake hit in 2010. Once the humor dissipates after listening to these disparate statements, one must become dead serious and understand why this may be a national threat for the United States of America, and a source of instability in the Western Hemisphere. Conducting research on news about Colombian guerrillas and narcotic trade incidentally forces a historic trip to investigate exactly what is involved when we talk about the "Movimiento Bolivariano" or "bolivarización." Simón Bolívar immediately comes to mind, and the historical background that always addressed the fact that Bolivar was the decisive factor, along with other great generals and leaders, in liberating South America from Spain's dominion.

Serving as an inspiration to Fidel Castro, Hugo Chavez, and a current wave of Latin American presidents, requires a look at Bolivar's proposal called "bolivarizacion," and the twists applied in the 21st century from a powerful emerging conglomerate that seems to siphon world superpower status from the motherly North Western Hemisphere's breasts to drip itself down into a wider crutch for the Southern Cone. Constantly keep in mind, however, that the objective in this text is to help YOU determine the value of legalizing drugs in the United States of America or the possibility of the global legalization of controlled substances. This initiative must address the known and unknown factors that must be linked to the most lucrative transnational business enterprise that has ever existed.

Simon Bolivar was instrumental in the independence movement against Spain, and we will revisit the public domain data available that portrays the values associated to the great leader. Bolivar's association with Western Hemisphere leaders led him to military strategies that forced the independence of many nations in South America. He was born in Caracas in 1783 to wealthy parents that died while he was still young, leaving him with a substantial fortune. Simon Bolivar received his education in Spain, and admired Napoleon I, but he also conducted studies on Rousseau, Locke, and Voltaire. These philosophers provided the infusion to believe a revolutionary movement in South America would succeed. There was a lot of inspiration from the philosophers that drove Bolivar to become energized with a desire to rebel against the Spaniards and seek independence. His exposure to the French and British ideas was finally injected with the United States of America's success in declaring its independence from the British.

Bolivar showed a desire to free the South American nations, as well as Central America and the Caribbean, from Spanish control. He was very rebellious and idealist, and saw the movement pro independence as a tool needed to restore the rights of the South American citizens in accordance to European beliefs. According to the Newsday Historical Digest and Scott Smith, fateful words from Alexander von Humboldt indicated that Bolivar's decision to bring independence to South America was at the proper moment, although van Humboldt was not sure at that point who would be the right person to lead the movement.

Bolivar felt empowered to lead the revolution with the military support and associations to Francisco de Miranda, Antonio José de Sucre, José de San Martín, and Bernardo O'Higgins. Their military strategies led to the successful liberation of South American nations from Spanish dominion. Once the process was completed, the Marquis de Lafayette sent a medallion recognizing Simón Bolívar as the South American counterpart to George Washington. Recognition for the success in liberating so many South American nations encouraged Simón Bolívar to believe his leadership would be instrumental in unifying Latin America parallel to the United States, an imitation leading to the creation of the United States of the Western Hemisphere.

His democratic belief that all men were created equal, however, was not exactly aligned to his belief that one day he would become the president for life of the united nations of the Western Hemisphere, resembling the European nations and the United States of America. This thought gave birth to the Twenty-First Century movement in Latin America recognized as "Movimiento Bolivariano" (Bolivarian Movement) or "bolivarización" (bolivarization), honoring the ideas of the great eighteenth Century leader. There are a few definitions of the term, which is based on Bolivar's idea to integrate all the Latin American nations as a conglomerate with shared leadership. Bolivar's success after leading the revolution in South America fell into disgrace as he ideologically supported, in a contradictory manner, monarchy and lifelong ruling similar to Fidel Castro's lifelong ruling privileges. His idea that all the nations liberated should be ruled by one "president;" that he should be that "president;" and that he would be able to rule all his life were the determining factors that brought a decline to his popularity. Leaders in the region opposed the "bolivarizacion" under these circumstances, due to its uncanny resemblance to a combined monarchy *quasi* dictatorship.

Simon Bolívar's idea to integrate the Western Hemispheric nations as a united group has acquired momentum in Latin America after more than a century, with a twisted version. Modeling after the United States and Europe has been replaced with networking with China, North Korea, Iran and Russia towards a nuclear proliferation process. Our theoretical legalization model, in addition, must explore how imminent trends indicate this emerging model of "bolivarización" may affect the national security of the United States of America, and hemispheric stability, if it is fully implemented based on the indicators available through leading actors of this process. The transnational leaders controlling illegal drug trade must definitely be taken into consideration, as legalization will have the most adverse impact against this business class. The symbiotic process between cartels, guerrillas, and illegal drug trade leads to the muscle behind illegal drug trade: the terrorist guerrillas funded by illegal narcotic trade, which I will call *narco-terrillas*.

Narco-terrilla groups representative of disruptive revolutionary movements in the region have been provided with weapons and supplies during the initial stages of the "Bolivarización" process. An increased acquisition of weapons, equipment, and military aircrafts in preparation for an "invasion" from the USA has been used as an excuse for weapons proliferation. Early inclusion of China to provide "technical advisors" in the region, along with open rhetorical attacks against US – Latin American policies, send a dynamic message that an investigation of this collusion will result in grave repercussions in regional security and, specifically threatened, the national security of the United States of America. Even if you believe that there is no relationship between the subject of this book and what you are now reading, you must follow through with how a historical movement begun in the 1800's will have a permanent impact on our decision whether controlled substances should be legalized.

Fidel Castro's efforts to impose the socialist-communist-Maoist agenda in the Western Hemisphere failed in the 1960's. Latin America's Stalin has succeeded at forging a new network of roots based on a twisted concept of "one nation with many presidents" as the latest version of "bolivarization." The leader responsible for manipulating diverse tools to achieve this goal has been Hugo Chavez, not Fidel Castro, who claims to have been Castro's mentee. The most important tool available to Chavez has been the financial resources available through the most resourceful South American OPEC nation: petrodollars. The financial wealth of the Venezuelan nation has been trickled down throughout the Western Hemisphere to readjust loyalty and empathy from capitalist ventures into socialized distribution of wealth. A distribution of petroleum to meet the needs of low income families throughout the hemisphere has provided expected results. State and national republics from Connecticut, USA to Argentina, SA have compromised their political character in behalf of the most dictatorial character emerging at the end of the Twentieth Century. Hugo Chavez' doctrine is likely to nurture the most revolutionary catastrophe in the first half of this century. His efforts have been masked under Simon Bolivar's initiatives dating back to the Nineteenth Century, and at some point he has indicated he is the resurrection of Simon Bolivar, which began to cast a shadow over this politician's mental health. In behalf of Chavez' apparent success, however, one must remember that Hitler was also considered insane at some point.

There are several definitions of the term "bolivarizacion." According to "Bolivarian Dreams" the term involves a "…consolidation of power under the leadership of one individual that exhibits populist characteristics." Among current Latin American leaders exhibiting these characteristics, we could name Fidel Castro, Hugo Chavez (Venezuela), Evo Morales (Bolivia), and Rafael Correa (Ecuador). We could also take into consideration nation orphan terrorist leaders such as Osama bin Laden, as well as organizations like the Taliban and Al-Qaeda. This "bolivarizacion" model portrays the movement as a political initiative with three different components:

1. central power focused on destroying the economic and political institutions
2. populist reform that provides benefits to the leadership
3. voting façade providing a false sense of democratic process in which the leadership maintains a lifelong post similar to the "caudillo"

Further research indicates that the term "bolivarizacion" is, according to DeBourbon,

" …a decidedly Marxist interpretation of some of the actions and views of *Simon Bolivar* during and immediately following his participation in the *South American Wars of Independence*" (2008).

Chavez interpretation casts conflicting ideas, as Bolivar's research models and exposure indicated as sources of inspiration the European and North American models for independence. Bolivar's belief in philosophies that recognize individual freedom and the fundamental rights of the citizens would be in altercation with Marxist beliefs in the class struggle. The independence movement in Latin America was precisely driven by the Latin American need to live with liberty, freedom, and the right to exist as an independent republic. Independence from Spain would not have been welcomed if it had included subjugation to another master ruler. However, it was also clear that Bolivar's idea to become the lifelong president of the unified "Bolivarian" nations was not a welcomed component to his brilliant military strategy. He believed in the value of a monarchy, which actually would run opposite to the principles involved in a socialist government. A look at Fidel Castro's system in Cuba shows an alignment with Bolivar's philosophy, where democratic electoral vote in Cuba includes nepotism when Castro appointed his brother as his successor, reminiscing of a monarchical line of heritage to the throne of a financially ruined economic system.

Among the issues driving the independence movements in Latin America, one must also take into consideration the fact that generations of creoles had begun to question Spain's dominion from a separate continent, void of a new culture that accommodated to different geo-political needs. Subjugation to an absent master due to intercontinental distance reinforced the model established by the USA's independence movement. Describing Bolivar as a socialist warrior in the class struggle, when he was actually a member of the aristocratic "criollos," is peculiar when considering Karl Marx's own writings on Bolivar, whom he dismissed as a false liberator who merely sought to preserve the power of the old Creole nobility to which he belonged. Falsifier, deserter, conspirator, liar, coward and looter are among the qualities used by Karl Marx when speaking about Simon Bolivar in 1858. Another contradiction from Chavez, the self proclaimed resurrection of Simon Bolivar, is his recent declaration in 2010 that he is a Marxist believer. This leads to a modification in what Chavez has called the Bolivarian revolution.

> "As tempting as it might be to think of Chávez as yet another demagogue taking advantage of the symbolic capital of a century and a half of Bolivarian nationalism, a closer look reveals that this president is engaged in a more complex transaction" (Conway 2003).

Even though there has been an orchestrated effort to link a leader of the revolution to a *de facto* global movement to destabilize global institutions in Latin America, the truth indicates that Venezuelan leadership is involved in the process of "Chavismo" instead of bolivarization. Chavez has acknowledged, according to CUBANET, that Cuba and Venezuela are one government with two presidents. They also claim that Chavez and Castro have expressed their desire to engage the USA in three or more Viet Nam conflicts. The current upsurge in socialist republics in Latin America has raised the question if Cuba, Venezuela, Ecuador, Bolivia, Chile, Argentina, and Nicaragua are actually one united government with several presidents.

The concept of one government with several presidents is probably a new trend Hugo Chavez may have compromised with to engage his Latin American homologous. This trend may be the initial stage of a process that will lead to the establishment of the United Socialist States of America, replicating Russia, and a response to the democratic United States of America. This would explain the measures taken by the government of Honduras to sever ties with their former president, based on the rhetorical threats indicating Venezuela was ready to invade Honduras to support the presidency of Manuel Zelaya. The reaction from the government of Honduras involved support from three separate branches of government empowered to protect their national security and preservation of their constitution: military enforcement expatriated Manuel Zelaya; the Honduran Congress provided the evidence indicating presidential violations to the Constitution; and the Supreme Court provided the legal enforcement. This process demonstrated the most assertive response against the process of "bolivarizacion."

Threats of a pending invasion from Venezuela to support Manuel Zelaya did not materialize for several reasons. The response from the government of the United States of America clearly stated misleading knowledge provided by the intelligence community in researching exactly what had transpired within the government of Honduras. A request to reinstall Manuel Zelaya was a clear indication that Washington, DC did not welcome collusion between Congress, the Supreme Court, and the Armed Forces to remove an elected president. The US Congressional Committee's visit to Tegucigalpa was responsible for publicly supporting the actions from the Honduran Government, detracting from the naïve notion from the US government that Zelaya should have been allowed to finish his term. In this case, The USG would have become instrumental in reinforcing the establishment of another "Bolivarian demo-tatorship" imitating Venezuela. A "demo-tatorship" is a term that could be used to identify the process of electing a president through democratic vote using democratic process, but mutating into a life-long dictatorship similar to Castro's model.

Hugo Chavez has led the march to resuscitate the bolivarization idea, and he believes he must be the leader charged with the geo-political transformation in the Western Hemisphere. Gang activities in major cities throughout the Western Hemisphere, sudden massive demonstrations of militant illegal immigrants, diplomatic relations between narco-terrorist groups and *de facto* governments, and the fact that terrorist sleeper cells momentum has failed to materialize need thorough and urgent research with the emerging unification of similar actors from Asia and the Middle East, whose common denominator to some Latin American countries is a global effort to destroy democratic systems. Research on the link between gangs and urban instability is focused on exploring how gang activity and urban guerrillas have linked their operations. Both groups are openly associated to illegal drug trade.

The link between different actors in the Western Hemisphere have been investigated in an effort to determine a vertical alignment of rhetorical threats, agreements and activities that may serve as indicators of terrorist events promoted under the emerging movement called "Bolivarización." The engine driving this movement continues to center around half a century efforts to force the global decline of the only superpower existing at this moment. However, the new superpower controlling transnational politics is a muscle operating under nations united and determined to distribute poverty equally between developing and developed nations. Efforts to reach national development based on the natural resources available in the geo-political scenario have moved to engage an international labor movement capable of decreasing production under the most incredible conditions forced upon humankind. It is crucial to recognize this movement and the global government it seeks to impose.

Recognition that a network had been developing was obvious as we looked into Pablo Escobar's connection to Raul Castro in the 1990's, who supposedly linked Colombian cartels exchanging Russian weapons with drugs as payments. It was a matter of time before the political guerrillas in Latin America began to provide security for the cartels. Evolution in the illegal drug trade is a fast paced enterprise that does not recognize boundaries. The Latin American guerrillas evolved into narco-guerrillas, a process which reinforced their agenda when they provided security for the cartels in exchange for drugs, enabling a permanent economic resource to supply their weapons and armaments trading drugs. Deeply engaged in studying this evolution led us to the reoccurring pronouncement asking for "bolivarizacion." The term had been hidden for over a century and a connection to Fidel Castro's mentee did not seem as an accurate link to the father of Latin America's independence movement in the twentieth century.

It is a surprise when research on illegal narcotics trade and terrorism, better known as narco-terrorism, became entangled with a movement that involved Simon Bolivar and his idea of a process known in the XIX century as "bolivarización." Research on the narcotics trade and guerrillas, or narco-guerrillas, along with their Marxist and/or Maoist policies has been an established and understandable connection. Support from the Cuban government and their socialist reform also seems to follow a natural reaction to the cause embraced by narco-guerrillas. Even the Irish Republican Army training connection to the Colombian guerrillas logically linked narco-guerrillas and terrorist movements. It is a defiant extension of historical truth to pretend the new movement linked to "Bolivarización" in the twenty-first century is rooted on the beliefs of the man that liberated South America from Spanish dominion. Nevertheless, many nations are now involved in the most lucrative business enterprise thanks to their political ancestral link

Decades of studies on narco-traffic evolvement brought countless sleepless nights as I feared the most bizarre connections to the financially successful illegal trade. The worst nightmares came as I finished my thesis on a Curriculum on Narcotraffic ©1998. In the 1990's we held discussions on how nuclear weapons would become one of the tools available to cartels and narco-trafficking groups. There was no doubt that narco-terrorism would be the most effective political tool in a *de facto* transnational government, trampling the philosophical boundaries that limit core and periphery issues in international politics.

CHAPTER III

NARCOTRAFFIC And The BOLIVARIAN WAR

The United States of America has been identified at the global level as having the largest appetite for drugs of such magnitude that, without any doubt, legalizing drugs in this country will have a transnational impact in the global economy. Several years ago, as a thesis project, I completed a curriculum on illegal drug trade to serve as an educational tool. The project was included in the International Criminal Investigative Training Assistance Program's (ICITAP) "Manual for Maritime Interdictions" designed under the supervision of Mike. ICITAP, a branch of the US Department of Justice, provided me with the practical experience to develop expertise in my field, as their assignments included developing and supporting law enforcement training programs in Bolivia, Honduras, Panama, El Salvador, and Colombia. These assignments provided first hand experience and knowledge validating this book, although research on the subject matter using electronic medium served to expand on the issues identified throughout Latin America and around the world. During the final development stages of the "**Colombian Unicurriculo**," funded by Plan Colombia in 2002, I found my curriculum project in the Bogota, Colombian office of ICITAP. Although I was never compensated financially for designing the curriculum, or for translating it to Spanish, it was clear that a **Curriculum on Narcotraffic** was essential to accurately address the organized networks involved in illegal drug trade. Sam B. Thibodeaux, a researcher of international politics and the Middle East, has provided her expertise expanding this research to other South American nations and their connections to the Middle East.

All the academic research we have conducted has been geared at understanding narcotraffic and the diverse components associated to illegal drug trade. Thibodeaux's research brings a political flair that merges the connection between Middle Eastern politics and narcotic trade. Our approach blends unusual instructional experience with academic knowledge on illegal drug trade, and the information you will receive by reading this book will provide you with current information on the process to strongly defend your vote, as we have no doubt that our nation will be casting a pro or contra vote on the issue of legalization within the coming decade. We have explained the engine behind the process of bolivarization, and must establish its link to narcotraffic. The basics on this trade follows, to help the reader understand the magnitude and universal approach generated by a highly sophisticated business. We will focus on Latin American illegal drug trade, beginning briefly with legalizing coca leaf products and ending with the marijuana crops.

Searching the Internet provides evidence that a movement to integrate crack cocaine and poppy products has begun its marketing stages with benefits that, according to promoters, must include them among the drugs that should be legalized using the same framework of "medicinal" value. USA President Barack Hussein Obama has already signed a bill that aims at reducing the sentences of those trafficking on cocaine. The concept that laws against crack-cocaine have penalized the black community in the USA served to support Obama's decision. This is a similar path that follows the marketing process to legalize marihuana in the 21st century. Doctors will prescribe marijuana as medicine in a process legalized or to be legalized in twenty five states, half of the states in the USA, as of August 2010.

Marihuana has also been known as "weed" because of its growth under any conditions in almost any environment. Harvesting and distribution in the states legalizing drugs has generated a new breed of businessmen marketing the product. Entrepreneur teachers of "Marihuana 101" courses on farming, harvesting, and marketing have emerged in a very competitive market. The sudden emergence of business enterprises associated to medicinal marihuana production have been tampering with bankruptcy and failed businesses because most people using the drug already have their resources, know how to grow "weed" in their own garden, and have abundant crops to use, consume and share. Half of the states in the United States, as of 2010, have either legalized medicinal marihuana consumption, or have pending legislation to legalize its use. Other crops and drugs, however, will remain illegal in the near future, but must be taken into consideration when we face the dilemma of which drugs provide "medicinal" value. The benefits achieved under legalization are recognized by the general population as the drop in arrests, crimes, and the violence linked to illegal drug trade. The arrest rates, as the violence we have suffered is mostly associated to the Latin American illegal narcotic trade or narcotraffic, should decline under this assumption. Our bordering nation, Mexico, has joined Colombia as the most violent countries, with criminal activity that indicates the establishment of a narcoterrorist state across the border from the USA. A porous frontier has shown the violence levels experienced in Colombia and Mexico has begun to seep into our southwestern states, labeling Phoenix, Arizona as the kidnapping capital in the world, an honor bestowed upon Colombia until 2010. A factor in our decision to legalize drugs must also be based, therefore, on knowledge about how this business operates and the advantages or disadvantages we will encounter as the legalization process is implemented.

Understanding narcotraffic must include an identification of the crops cultivated for the trade. This segment, therefore, will not include issues related to methamphetamine or opium derivatives. Recognition of the producing and consumer nations is important because it will provide knowledge on the issues that maintain peripheral nations from developing their natural resources. There is so much information available through electronic medium that inclusion of the basic steps and stages in production of illegal drugs is no longer a threat to our national security when published in textbooks. Actually, most of this information is basic and accessible through electronic medium. However, this bit of information that has become accessible through public domain helps to understand the chemical components affecting consumers of illegal drugs. A link between bolivarization and narcotraffic will be available to understand the importance of this movement in the crucial process of legalizing drugs in the USA.

The most important producing nations involved in the crack-cocaine business are Bolivia, Peru, and Colombia, with Ecuador's recent attempts to join the business. Bolivia and Peru have been the main producers of coca leaves, with Colombia ranking as a distant third producing nation. The quality of the coca leaves produced in Bolivia and Peru is of higher quality than that of Colombian coca. Colombia's specialty, however, is in the chemical process in permanent and mobile laboratories to finish the product for distribution, as well as the trafficking segment of the business. Bolivia and Peru have suffered from development restrictions because they are the raw material suppliers in this deal. The advantage these nations have is that coca leaf production requires two geographical elements that cannot be recreated elsewhere: the altitude levels and low temperatures offered by the Andean mountain range combined with the humidity generated by the Amazonian region. The administrative savvy from the Colombian Cartels developed and marketed the main crop used in Andean rituals into an illegal transnational marketing enterprise.

The process to empower the cartels would not have been possible without the efforts in the USA to make cocaine an illegal product. A quick history of how cocaine became illegal will date back to the 1800's when it was used around the world as a tonic with medicinal powers. A German chemist, Friedrich Gaedcke, was able to isolate the alkaloids in the coca leave around 1855. By the end of the century serious issues had been recognized associated to cocaine, although scientists like Sigmund Freud consumed the product and prescribed it to others in an incredible effort to control opium addiction through the use of cocaine. The use of cocaine as medication was later mass produced and introduced with the famous "COCA"-Cola tonic, which was among one of the factors that led to the creation of the Food and Drug Administration and the Drug Enforcement Agency. In 1922 the USA government had identified cocaine as a dangerous drug for human consumption. However, the medicinal value from coca leaf extracts were recognized and are still used legally in some types of prescribed and over the counter medication regulated by the FDA and produced by regulated laboratories.

The illegal laboratory process to change coca leaves into crack-cocaine products involve the use of certain chemicals that are not normally used for human consumption. The chemicals include sulfuric acid, types of chloride and ether, benzoate, ammonia, and kerosene. Most people in their right mind will not engage in ingesting or inhaling these chemicals into their system because of lethal effects. A visual image I have used to help young people understand the impact suffered by coca leaves, a natural ritualistic native product, into an illegal mind altering drug, is its conversion from a green leaf into a white rock or powder base using the basic detergent for bleaching. The Andean indigenous tribes use, instead, natural grain such as burned quinoa as a precipitating agent. The nations producing the raw material growing coca leaves, used in Latin American Andean rituals, must depend on the chemicals developed by industrialized nations to process the natural product into a marketable illegal drug. The use of poisonous chemicals to market the coca by-products around the world should help create some type of consciousness as to the final objective behind this market. In addition, this dependency forces the status of developing nations, formerly known as underdeveloped countries, to remain at a level in which they cannot compete in the global market to generate, manufacture, or advance their technology to compete in a *de juro* global economy. One could conclude that the indigenous groups in Latin America and the American public have been brought into an economic war and level of self destruction by obscure forces we have not been able to identify.

The level of addiction that has evolved in the USA, the illegal status of drugs, and the Latin American nations' failure to establish governments geared to support diversification through free enterprise create a socio-economic and political frame that deprives the Western Hemisphere from development and modernization. In addition, dependence on the underground economy generated through illegal trade forces the population to stagnate its development due to an immensely profitable economic process that, legally, does not exist. Illegal drugs, in essence, have become a dictatorial regime in which the agricultural economy forces segments of the population to remain subservient to militant few using violence and power to control natural resources. Multinational operations related to narcotraffic, such as the chemical providers, depend on this market to maintain their profits; while they pretend to be blind admitting illegal trade could not survive without support from independent corporations that sell these chemicals to shell corporations.

Networks operating these shells in Miami, Puerto Rico, and Colombia serve pool and industrial cleaner businesses that later pass the chemicals down to cartel laboratories. Before 9/11, anti-narcotic operatives had identified oil and petroleum companies in Mexico delivering these chemicals throughout Central America. The military and law enforcement agencies throughout the region provided escort and protection services to guarantee prompt delivery using a similar system as the "Federal Express," an uninterrupted process flowing freely at a transnational level. Building the Pan American Highway, for example, served to facilitate the delivery system needed by the cartels to transport drugs illegally throughout Latin America. The summer of 2010 brought recognition that over 100,000 trained Mexican soldiers had changed rank to serve the cartels for a better salary. Believing that this identifies the Mexican government as unethical and corrupt is only the tip of the iceberg as Latin American governments from one tip of the continent to the other suffer from the same malady. The Honduran military is notorious for its high level of corruption. Transportation of illegal drugs from Venezuela, for example, was possible before 9/11 due to the escort service provided by some corrupt law enforcement and military personnel.

The cartels and narcoguerrillas, among others, depend on this market to maintain their income levels and survive financially. These characters, from farmers to kingpins, need addicts to continue buying illegal drugs, and benefit from drug addiction growth throughout the world. Intense marketing and distribution aimed at generating a world of addicts is needed to fuel the market with more addicts, which continuously prefer to target USA citizens. The old adage that narcotraffic exists due to the USA's appetite for illegal drugs may show another side of a coin: the creation of a market targeting Americans. We, the USA citizens, have enjoyed the benefits from the superpower national status since the end of the Cold War. The last quarter of the Twentieth Century brought development and financial wealth that eventually created targets of our men and women. This level of abundance at a global level created resentment among citizens of nations still in developing stages.

Hugo Chavez' Bolivarization process, for example, has been concentrating his efforts for almost a decade to empower presidents like Evo Morales in attempts to legalize coca leaf production. Efforts to legalize coca leaf production in Latin America have been fruitless when we compare the issues associated to societal development. During a conversation in 1997 with agents from the Federal Bureau of Investigations (FBI), we all agreed that the USA government's eradication efforts are not geared to interfere with centuries of rituals and traditions established in the Andean region, but rather to drive Latin America through socio-economic reforms to develop their natural resources and become a competitive productive force. This is the war on narcotraffic from the societal development standpoint. Financial subsidies from the Bolivian government to the famous "Cholas" in Bolivia, which are the equivalent of street vending businesswomen in La Paz, would become ultimately more productive than providing rural farmers with the legal incentive to plow six hectares of coca instead of two. The first will encourage citizens to create products for marketing and enhance an industry; the second continues an agricultural saga where overproduction will bring down the price of raw material in a violent illegal global market, eventually forcing the farmer to pay additional protection taxes to the narcoguerrillas because more hectares will be farmed. The new breed of Castro clones throughout the hemisphere will continue to provide multiple stagnant economies throughout Latin America.

Following through the issues involved with narcotraffic we have explored how we have nations plowing the land for raw material (Bolivia, Peru, and rural Colombia) while Colombians profit for decades with a global distributorship of crack cocaine to transit nations. The farmer's pay is a misery, as well as the middlemen, when we compare it to the billions of dollars generated by the cartels. Even though we are faced in the first decades of the 21st century with the worst financial global disaster, the Latin American narcotrafficking nations have an underground economy supporting their nations financially, mostly thanks to our addicted population in the USA. All nations are part of a production, processing, distribution, transiting, and/or consumption network of illegal drugs. Those claiming that the war on drugs has been a failure lack understanding on how the Drug Enforcement Administration (DEA), along with all other law enforcement agencies have succeeded in other areas. Their success level, however, has created a mutating impact that has forced narcotrafficants to transmute into the most incredible global force capable of incredible instant diversification. The effectiveness of our drug enforcement agencies provides the cartels with a constant level of accelerated creativity and motivation. The effectiveness of our law enforcement agencies, therefore, has been the indirect catalyst element that contributes to the eternal cartel diversification process.

The heroin market had been long established before cocaine and marihuana came into the competitive marketplace. British and Europeans were targeted specifically, as a military strategy against European superpowers, to create the heroin addiction market. This led European governments to create laws identifying heroin and poppy products as illegal. Cartels in Mexico and Venezuela, among other nations, have succeeded at producing poppy and marketing heroin and other byproducts to the USA because it had been nearly impossible to penetrate and compete with the Colombian cartel's crack-cocaine market. The production of coca leaves requires the appropriate temperature from high altitudes, as well as the humidity levels from the Amazon area. The coca producing nations, regardless of the billions generated through illegal drug trade, remain at developing levels. The geography and topography forced the world to deal with the Colombian Cartels, successful in marketing and creating an illegal industrialized subculture, generating at some point the need for protection from contract mercenaries called "sicarios."

Since prosecution against "sicarios" was strictly enforced by the Colombian judicial system plus they had to face stiff sentences, the business resorted to hiring "young sicarios," which are adolescents and young people paid to commit murders mostly by riding in motorcycles. An advantage to hiring young "sicarios" was that it forced a moral dilemma in the judicial system when judgment sentences involved juveniles committed to life in prison. The Cartels' strategy succeeded, as juvenile sentencing provided the cartels with a criminal revolving door lasting generations. It maximized the sicarios productivity to a lifelong profitable criminal career with death benefits, as the kingpins provided their mourning families with monetary rewards. As a business enterprise, it provided Colombian criminals with a paid career from age 13 until death, an economic resource unmatched by government or private sources that eventually forced the deterioration of the poor and existing middle class family structure at the expense of financial rewards in exchange for violent mercenary acts.

Anti-narcotic efforts began to show success, and about the same time period the rural area farmers were levied taxes by the guerrillas to keep military and national law enforcement agencies at a distance from the coca farms. The success achieved by the DEA was the main driving motivation that drove the cartels to pay exorbitant amounts for protection. Pablo Escobar's policies to seek protection from possible informants included subsidizing home construction for his followers; and also providing payments to purchase homes, automobiles, and comfort prohibitive to Colombia's poor and middle class. The class levels struggled and suffered throughout Latin America due to the stagnant socio-economic development, as well as vindictive politics, which contributed to the support for the "get-rich-quick" schemes offered through narcotraffic. The Colombian Cartels controlled the crack-cocaine global market and became the envy of organized crime organizations, which enriched Colombia's *de facto* economy. The Cartel envoys established contacts in Russia, the Middle East, and Cuba and remained in control due to the coca leaves strategic growing location, blessing the illegal trade with a controlled market.

Pablo Escobar's death marked a new era for the Cartels where a stronger force based on principles and ideals was needed for protection. The infrastructure established by the cartels had been exposed and was finally infiltrated. Cali, Medellin, and the Atlantic Cartels all suffered from turf wars, but were finally shaken in part due to their fragile illegal infrastructure. The unprecedented alliance between cartels and guerrillas provided the cartels with temporary loyalty, as it was highly unlikely for the guerrillas to provide the government with any information about the cartels. The symbiosis merged the ruthlessness of the revolutionary movements in Colombia with the illegal Cartel infrastructure, at the same time weakened the financial fortress built by the Cartels, siphoning the funds in an unexpected move from narcoguerrillas. Narcotraffic sought assistance from the guerrilla movements that have contributed to maintain Colombia in a state of war for almost half a century.

At this point we have to introduce briefly the original Colombian guerrillas linked to narcotics trade, which are the Frente Armado Revolucionario Colombiano (FARC) or Colombian Revolutionary Armed Front; the Ejercito de Liberación Nacional (ELN) or National Liberation Army; and the Autodefensas Unidas Colombianas (AUC) United Colombian Auto defense. The FARC is associated to a communist rural agenda and receives medical and political support from the Cuban and Venezuelan government. The ELN is a Marxist organization originally based on liberation theology principles, contrary to Marxist atheism, of equal distribution of wealth, and has declared itself recently as an urban guerrilla movement following Che Guevara's ideals. The AUC is a paramilitary group, linked to the Colombian military structure, originally set to destroy narcotrafficking networks and the guerrilla groups. They later degenerated into another guerrilla group using narcotics, transporting them, and cashing on the trade to support their rank. In 2008 many of them turned their weapons to the Colombian government and faced prosecution and/or reintegration based on similar "pentiti" principles like those applied to the Red Brigades in Italy. The evolution that brought a merge between the cartels and the guerrillas gave birth to the *narcoguerrillas* which were originally revolutionary movements used by illegal narcotic groups for protection. Protection from these groups proved to be almost a blessing for the cartels, until greed led the guerrillas to other arrangements.

The narcoguerrillas association to the cartels was originally as a source of protection. The farmers were protected from military and law enforcement government intrusion. The laboratories processing coca to paste received other types of protection from military and law enforcement intervention to guarantee uninterrupted processing. The middlemen received protection transporting their products from the labs to their transit points. Cartel members also received protection, as well as their families. This led the guerrillas to understand the process used from planting to selling, and they were able to impose their own "tax" system at all levels of illegal drug trade against all people involved. Incidentally, seeking protection served to shake the cartels control by transforming the revolutionary movements into an educated group on the illegal drug trade, forming what we know as the narcoguerrillas. The narcoguerrillas have diluted the cartel controls and at the same time have been able to fund their training and connections with a global political network that includes Venezuela, Cuba, the Irish Republican Army, Hezbollah, China, Russia, North Korea, Iran, and the Middle East.

These connections, discussed in depth in another chapter, indicate how we are dealing with more than just the illegal drug trade, yet do not bring together the connection between the "Bolivarian War" and narcotraffic. Another factor taken into consideration when we try to understand narcotraffic is the money laundering process that has created a global *de facto* economy. Money laundering is the process in which funds, in this case illegal, are transferred through sophisticated methods to give the appearance that the funds have been obtained through a legal process of labor and hard work. Tracking laundered money is not an easy task, and the selected few that benefit from the process are likely to include, among others, most of the business people and corrupt politicians that refuse to consider legalization as an option. It is quite possible, however, that they will consider legalization as soon as they can engage in establishing the business operation apparatus that will funnel money back into their pockets. Legalizing marihuana in California, for example, generated a new breed of small business entrepreneurs who were immediately put out of business in less than a year. The emerging transnational enterprises promptly established state of the art production of marihuana at an industrialized level, leading to the assumption that politicians and functioning transnational farming groups had been preparing for the mass production of legalized marihuana crops.

These individuals and corporations are likely to be the same elements that had cushioned themselves under legalized enterprises difficult to identify during the illegal drug business status. Right before this book was submitted for publishing, new information surfaced to support our analysis. It is no coincidence that the AFL-CIO has announced its intention to represent and "unionize" the marijuana farmers of the world months before the US Congress concludes its study on legalizing drugs. This announcement came, also, weeks after announcements that Oakland [California] will begin factory produced medical marijuana.

Plans to provide loans to subsidize such farms are under consideration in California, including the consideration that the farms may produce marijuana for recreational purpose. The segment of the American public that refuses to consider legalization as an option, however, are your average educated conservatives with knowledge on the adverse physiological effects caused by drug use, also knowledgeable of nurturing and assertive behavior modification practices that substitute chemical dependency with self-reliability.

Thibodeaux's technical analysis supports these premises, and establishes a common ground between the northern and southern countries in South America. Money laundering, corruption and narcotics trafficking are interrelated. The National Anti-Drug Secretariat of Paraguay suggests that "narcotic trafficking generates approximately 40% of the laundered funds" in the Triple Border Area (TBA) that includes Paraguay, Brazil, and Uruguay. It is also suggested that the officials who are responsible for combating corruption are the same ones that are facilitating money laundering (Sverdlick, 2005, p. 88). Ignoring corrupt states is at the peril of the international community. Corrupt states are "incubators of terrorism, the narcotics trade, money laundering, human trafficking, and other global crime-raising issues far beyond corruption" (Heimann and Heinemann, 2006). Corrupt officials and politicians have "...used the black market to transmit their illegally obtained wealth" ("Brazilian Politician Charged with Theft of Over 11 Million Dollars," 2007). We should assume that legalization, therefore, will eliminate the corrupt states, which in turn will eliminate terrorism, money laundering, human trafficking, and other global criminal activity related to illegal drug trade.

The Colombian guerrillas are not the only ones reaping a profit from illegal drug trade. It is estimated that between US$300 million and US$500 million in profits is sent from the TBA every year from fundamentalist groups in this area to Islamic groups in the Middle East. These profits come from "drug trafficking, arms dealing, and other illegal activities including money-laundering, contraband, and product piracy" (Hudson, 2003, p. 4). The profits are easily transferred, "...with lax border controls and more than 100 hidden airstrips in the region" (Hudson, 2003, p. 24). According to public media reports the amount of currency brought into the country is without limits and at the same time does not require any type of financial disclosure when crossing the border. The facilities provided through ease of financial transactions are indicators of money laundering safe haven practices in Paraguay. This lack of accountability provides the establishment of shell corporations and transactions that have been in place to funnel illegal drug financial transactions. The final objective of these groups such as the Colombian Atlantic, Cali, and Medellin cartel members had been to funnel these funds to bring their wives, children, and themselves into the world of successful entrepreneurs. These groups want to generate money; however, cartels and revolutionary movements seek different objectives. The narcoguerrillas want the money to subsidize their revolutionary movement agenda. Their final interest is to support their agenda, goals, and objectives using funding from illegal drugs. Their purchasing power in the black market requires payments in cash that cannot be traced.

The narcoguerrillas, groups of outlaw like cartel members, and states harboring terrorism have a political goal to use such funding to destabilize governments. Merging the guerrillas with the process of Bolivarization expands the local objectives from a controlled centralized location into a hemispheric destabilization process. Politically, the Bolivarization process needs the funding and muscle to fight the wars capable of "liberating" the Latin American nations and unite them under one president. A call for unity from Venezuelan president Hugo Chavez seeks to form one hemispheric nation with several presidents. This concept is actually the same effort that led to the creation of the European Union, which is an apparent modernized version of Simon Bolivar's concept. President Chavez, however, has harbored the Colombian narco-guerrilla groups and has provided the connections used to support revolutionary movements through South, Central America, and the Caribbean. The Colombian Cartel's infrastructure has been absorbed in many ways by the narcoguerrillas which seem to have relegated the cartels into an administrative global position while they delegate control of the operational national and or continental aspect of the business among Marxist-Communist guerrillas. In exchange, the funds generated by the narcoguerrillas are substantially used to develop the bellicose machinery needed by the bolivarization process.

Hugo Chavez contributions to the Summit of the Americas, and his leadership in establishing the process of bolivarization, have served to detract the USA's influence in the Western Hemisphere. Efforts to establish the Free Trade Agreement of the America's have stagnated as Venezuelan petrodollars have been used to influence, infiltrate, and persuade the Latin American voters against what Chavez calls USA interference in Latin American affairs. However, Bolivarization was the main cause cited by the Honduran Congress, military forces, and Supreme Court in their decision to oust President Manuel Zelaya and send him to Costa Rica in 2009. In depth research on the subject indicates President Zelaya's alliance to the process of Bolivarization was in developmental stages. Following similar strategies imposed in Venezuela, Zelaya was in the process of violating constitutional law to preserve his presidency beyond term limits using the popular Cuban-Venezuelan system of voting democratically for the one and only legitimately proposed candidate in the ballot. The Honduran electoral ballots to be used had been printed in, no other than, Venezuela, infringing in the affairs of a sovereign nation. Hugo Chavez had activated the Venezuelan Army to protect Zelaya's plan, however, the decisions from the Honduran Congress and Supreme Court were efficiently implemented before Chavez could bring Venezuelan troops into Honduras. The Organization of American States, as well as the ambivalence from the USA government's self restraint to interfere, served to cast doubt in the Venezuelan government's decision to launch a full fledged attack to reinstate Zelaya back in power.

Chavez staged a coupe d'état in 1993, while I was working as a consultant in Panama, which brought a massive movement from all branches of surrounding governments and created serious questions as to how far Chavez was willing to go to control the government. Knowing his personality, the Panamanian people were also concerned if his attack would be limited to the Venezuelan country. His failed attack at that time was a clear message from the Venezuelan people. The people's response forced him to slow down his ambition and efforts to control his country, but it also showed he had some military support and aggressiveness capable of destabilizing Venezuela plus bordering nations. The military dictatorship methods used in 1993 were an early reminder of his political intentions, using brutal force if necessary under a democratic system where elections are a "rule of law." The last few years have demonstrated his determination to establish the Bolivarian Republic has been partially successful. Through his leadership, Latin America has regressed to establish the largest amount of socialist led republics similar to the era when Che Guevara and Fidel Castro attempted to export socialism throughout the Western Hemisphere. Instability in the northern nations in South America, through threats from the guerrilla groups linked to narcotraffic, is at a dangerous level because the funds generated through illegal drug trade are used to subsidize massive trade in weapons for the guerrilla movements. Venezuela and Cuba have served as intermediaries in the connections, trade, storage, and delivery of these supplies and weapons. Ecuador and Venezuela have all harbored the FARC and ELN, continuing to force the perpetual instability in Colombia. The most disturbing aspect of this interference is the links established among guerrilla groups, states harboring terrorist groups, and the global networks supported by illegal drug trade.

Venezuela is one of Colombia's bordering nations, as well as Ecuador, Brazil, Peru, and Panama. An educator I met before providing consultant work for Plan Colombia expressed her frustration because the rural communities in Colombia were harassed by the military and law enforcement, accusing them of harboring and supporting guerrilla groups. At the same time, the guerrillas forced taxes on the farmers and accused them of providing information about the guerrillas to the militaries and the National Police. This left the rural communities feeling they were "alone," unprotected by the government and haunted by the guerrillas. The instability created under these circumstances has provided the fuel needed to support Chavez' initiatives in the hemisphere. His promise to distribute wealth and provide hemispheric security under the Bolivarian Republic has attracted the attention of all the Latin American nations. The USA, the only nation recognized with superpower status in the world until the 2010 financial crisis, has been advertised as incapable of providing security against the illegal drug groups or the political corruption in the region, thus leaving few other options available to establish the links needed to develop such protection within Latin American nations. The Drug Enforcement Agency, along with anti-narcotic law enforcement agencies in the region, have been forced to operate against drug trade single handed facing multiple issues that revolve around addressing terrorist activities, transnational arm trade, human trafficking, civil unrest, socio-economic problems, and weapons of mass destruction.

An ingredient the citizens in these nations have failed to factor in is that such instability has been nurtured, developed, and created by the same actor claiming to be the only solution to rational cohesiveness in the Western Hemisphere. Once the guerrillas merged with the Colombian Cartels, they were able to generate enough economic resources to support the military strategies required to impose the revolution. The Bolivarization process, supported by Hugo Chavez, established the connections needed to provide technical advisors and training using global resources and the use of weapons, as well as technical advisors for the narco-guerrillas. The ideas generated by Simon Bolivar to unite Latin American countries have been expanded to include the Marxist, Socialist, Maoist, and/or Communist inclinations exhibited by the Latin American rebel and guerrilla groups. Once again, we have seen the survival and resurrection of militant groups under a new umbrella claiming to bring reforms to the hemisphere under the disguise of authentic ideas generated by Bolivar. Bolivar, in a contradictory tone, may have recognized democracy and capitalism as the tools needed to generate development and the free enterprise needed to shape Latin America into the world of fully developed nations contributing at the global core.

Venezuela's marketing of the Bolivarization Movement (BM), however, has used the resources generated through illegal drug trade to disguise the developmental establishment of hegemonic totalitarian rule throughout the northern countries in South America, with a clear impact throughout the Western Hemisphere. Colombia, of all nations, has first-hand experience trying to stabilize their nation from the mutating evolution process imposed by guerrillas under the guidance of Venezuela's government. Even though there is a dispute between both governments, the evidence available through the impact suffered in Colombia's socio-economic/political development is a reality. Disputes with Ecuador, which had aligned efforts with Chavez' bolivarization movement, provided evidence that the movement based within the governments of Cuba and Venezuela are aligned to a new hemispheric hegemony. This may be, as Chavez indicates, one nation with many presidents. Or, it may end up being the demise of many nations under one Bolivarian president likely to be Hugo Chavez, with Raul and Fidel Castro's blessing. Chavez has a narcissist personality that needs to be nurtured and cultivated to make him the center of attention. His mentor, Fidel Castro, has mellowed down under the "father figure," indicating Cuba is likely to be presented to the world as the First Bolivarian Republic under many presidents led by, none other than, Hugo Chavez. This may lead his brother, Raul Castro, to perform his first act of sibling rivalry and defiance if he decides to pull the carpet from under Chavez' feet.

Venezuela's interfering support for the Colombian guerrillas was officially admitted after several computers with electronic evidence were found among the FARC's belongings during a Colombian incursion into Ecuador. Protests from the Ecuadorian government rightfully claimed interference with their rights as a sovereign nation. Colombian officials made it clear, however, that the guerrilla groups established in a remote militant base had fled from Colombian borders, justifying their incursion into Ecuador. Evidence indicated this was an established Colombian guerrilla base networking from Ecuador. Significant information in the computers confiscated by the Colombian government shed light on the involvement and profound implications connecting Venezuelan officials to the FARC's operations as a revolutionary movement. The establishment of several US military bases in Colombia was supported and reinforced by the Colombian people as evidence indicated the transnationalization of a complex movement was aimed at the Colombian nation. Efforts had been consolidated between subversive groups, terrorist states, and a blend of transnational collusion led by Hugo Chavez. The last decade has served to establish there has been a connection between the government of Hugo Chavez, the ELN, and the FARC. The connection has served to strengthen and protect revolutionary movement operations in South America. The USA's support to enter the militant FARC base in Ecuador provided needed evidence to denounce narcoguerrilla expansion into other South American borders, supported by the Venezuelan government.

There is no evidence that Hugo Chavez is using the narcoguerrillas to advance his Bolivarian war. There is evidence that he is harboring and supporting Colombian guerrillas, which presents an obligation to question the ulterior motive this president has in protecting groups of outlaw revolutionaries responsible for destabilizing and interfering with other sovereign nations. The summer of 2010 has brought more visible connections between Hugo Chavez and the Colombian and Mexican Cartels. Troubling as it may sound for the national security of the United States, other links have surfaced establishing a direct association between Chavez and a Hezbollah presence in the frontier between Mexico and the USA. Developing news at this time is indicating Hezbollah's intention to establish bases in the Western Hemisphere are financed with cocaine profits.

Thibodeaux's assertion of a connection between narcotraffic and terrorist groups is a reality connecting narcotraffic with Middle Eastern terrorist organizations. Looking back at how the cocaine business has expanded, at one point South American law enforcement had received intelligence information showing Muslim representatives were seeking to purchase cocaine from the cartels. Their intention was to taint the cocaine with arsenic and sell it in the USA. Serious consideration was given to the idea; however, the Cartel's would have lost their reliability and business with American addicts, as all the sources would have come from the Western Hemisphere. The Muslim representatives could have tainted heroin based products, which would have likely blamed mostly the Middle East as attempting against American lives, adding a new tactic to "terrorist" attacks. Mexico and Venezuela have also engaged in poppy production for over a decade, and would have been under the scope along with the Middle East. Even though the reliability of certain intelligence sources could not be established, at one point we were aware that human trafficking in 2003 included illegal immigrants from Middle Eastern nations. It was August 2010, however, when the USA government acknowledged intelligence gathering sources were accurately identifying human smuggling included Middle Eastern members of Hezbollah. During the last ten years, illegal immigrants of Middle Eastern descent have been entering the country passing as Latin Americans. Intelligence reports from reliable sources continue to indicate individuals of Muslim descent continue to enter the USA mingling with Latin American illegal immigrants. The issue of identity theft may have more serious implications than we have been led to believe.

Thibodeaux's analysis on other South American nations deserves serious consideration, as she ties a loop between events from the 1990's to the Middle East and Latin American events developing at this time. According to Thibodeaux, the Triple Border Area (TBA) in Latin America has been known for illegal activities that deserve further investigation leading our research into an amazing global connection. This region, located where Argentina, Brazil and Paraguay meet, lacks truly effective border controls, which facilitates smuggling of goods and humans. The area has been known as a transit zone for illegal drugs. It had never been a region of vital interest to the United States until the attack on September 11, when the United States was forced to examine Islamic terrorist organizations and countries that pose threats to the national security of the United States. Two events in the early 1990s aroused suspicion leading the United States to examine this region for potential Islamic terrorist threats (Faiola, 2001).

In March 1992, the Israeli Embassy in Argentina was attacked by a suicide bomber, which killed 29 people and wounded 135 others. Originally, a group known as "Pro-Palestine," and later the group known as Islamic Jihad, claimed responsibility for the attacks, but there was no confirmation of who was responsible ("Argentina Asks Interpol to Arrest Hezbollah Leader," 2002). A military Hezbollah commander had been killed by Israeli forces before the attack (Connell, 2006). Because of the large Arab population in this region between the three countries, this attack on the Israeli Embassy was seen as retaliation by Lebanese supporters. Two years later, in July 1994, it was speculated that a suicide bomber for Hezbollah was responsible for the detonation of a van outside the Argentina Israelite Mutual Association in Buenos Aires (McDonnell, 2006). It was suggested that "Iran's top leaders were motivated to order the bombing by Argentina's decision in 1992 to cut off its supply of nuclear materials to Iran." However, Argentina and Iran were still having negotiations over the issue when both the bombings happened (Porter, 2006). Moshen Rabbani, an Iranian Embassy attaché in Argentina, was accused by officials in the Argentina government of "having provided logistical assistance to Hezbollah elements that entered Argentina illegally" through the TBA to carry out the 1994 bombing ("Argentina Asks Interpol to Arrest Hezbollah Leader," 2002). This is just one of several examples of alleged ties between the TBA and terrorist organizations.

The Triple Border Area (TBA) where Brazil, Argentina, and Paraguay meet is a region suffering from money laundering, narcotics trafficking, and piracy of computer software and music (Sverdlick, 2005, p.88). The three cities involved heavily in these illegal activities are Ciudad del Este in Paraguay, Foz de Iguazu in Brazil, and Puerto Iguazu in Argentina. Ciudad Del Este is Paraguay's second largest city. According to Hudson (2003: 6-8) "Arabic is heard as much as, or perhaps more than, Spanish" in this city. Ciudad Del Este is an alleged safe-haven for Islamic terrorists, and "a major transshipment point for drugs, not to mention a center of black market commerce" (Pion-Berlin, 2000, p. 56). The Pan American Highway runs through this city connecting it to Curitiba, Brazil. Foz de Iguazu is one of Brazil's most violent cities, and was reported in the Overseas Security Advisory Council as having selected gang group activities similar to those conducted by terrorist groups. This, in itself, is an issue of great interest in the next chapter, and must be kept in mind. Ninety percent of the Arab population (with a rough estimate of 30,000 people) in Ciudad Del Este and Foz de Iguazu is Lebanese (Hudson, 2003, p. 8). Puerto Iguazu, Argentina does not have any Arab or Jewish communities (Sverdlick, 2005, p. 85).

Thibodeaux's research included the assertion that at the time of these events drug trafficking, corruption and money laundering were not considered to have a direct impact on the United States security in the way that terrorism had, and could possibly be handled by the three countries involved. The presence of a Lebanese population in this region raised alarm with the countries fighting the War on Terrorism, particularly the United States. A major issue had been whether the United States was discriminating against this region by targeting it simply because of its Arab population, or whether there was enough evidence to support the claim that Hezbollah, a Lebanese organization whose militant wing conducts terrorist activities throughout the world and is supported by the Iranian regime, conducts financing operations and/or terrorist operations in this area (Byman, 2003). The operations that needed to be examined at the time were whether they had an operating base in this area, and whether they were receiving funds from the illegal activities such as money laundering and narcotics trafficking. At that time it was also analyzed the effect MERCOSUR, the Common Market of the South, had on the illegal activities that affect the region on the borders of these three countries.

Honduras has another Lebanese community that had been under investigation in the 1990's. Working for the Ministerio Publico in 1999, the equivalent of the US Attorney General's Office, offered an unusual opportunity which put this community under a different perspective. Rumors of a possible attack during the 2000 millennium celebrations had spread throughout the USA, with intelligence gathering providing similar results. Information had surfaced after the Russian block had collapsed that suitcases with nuclear material had disappeared, or were unaccounted. The location of this material indicated several third world nations were seeking to purchase the material. According to some unnamed official with the government, Italian mobsters had delivered one of the suitcases to a member of the Honduran community. The delivery man had contacts with the government to enter the country without any problems. At the same time, news of a "chinaso" had been made public.

The Honduran government, known to be the most corrupt government in the Western Hemisphere, had been selling Honduran nationalities indiscriminately to citizens of China, therefore giving birth to the term "chinaso." After the Chinese were nationalized, they were also sold passports to enter the USA. Honduran citizens working in the American Embassy in Honduras were responsible for guaranteeing these passports for a substantial fee. While shopping at a beauty shop in North Carolina, I asked the Oriental looking nice lady where she was from, expecting her to answer the name of a Pacific Islander or Eastern nation. She answered she was from Honduras, which led me to ask her a million questions in Spanish that she could not answer. She was unable to answer because I was asking her in Spanish and she could not speak Spanish. A couple of years after that I was at the post office finalizing a message when I noticed a "Sumo wrestler" looking young man followed a young Asian into the office. He had left his Yukon SUV running while escorting her into the building. Out of her large pocketbook she pulled out wads of dollars, and purchased money orders which totaled over $8,000. Federal law requires bank disclosure of citizens that engage in monthly dollar transactions exceeding $10,000 per month. However, money laundering efforts may be able to succeed with other sources such as your local post office.

The connection I tried to establish in this case, however, involved the case of an illegal immigrant acquaintance who had entered the country pregnant and claiming to be years younger than she actually was. While waiting to go into a movie theater, the young lady arrived with members of her family. Her supposedly older brother was unable to utter any words in neither English nor Spanish, and his physical appearance did not seem to be of the same tone or physique as his sister. This proved to be curious but of no concern to me until 9/11. Her brother had an uncanny resemblance to one of the terrorists, Muhammad Atta. Among the data offered by reliable sources, claims of people that have entered the USA illegally through Mexico include Middle East citizens. The picture that I clearly remembered then was that of my acquaintance's brother, and how the physical appearance of Middle Eastern natives and Latin Americans is very similar, especially if they do not speak at all. A raid conducted in August 2010 resulted in the arrest of members from Hezbollah trying to establish a training camp near the border region between Mexico and the USA. A large cache of weapons was confiscated at the same time, as well as cash. The reader should keep in mind that these incidents indicate a relationship has been established between elements from the Middle East linked to terrorist organizations, human trafficking and organized crime. Keep in mind, also, that there are over seven million individuals in Latin America of either Lebanese, Syrian or Palestinian origin. One million of them live in Brazil, and another million lives in Argentina. Both Brazil and Argentina are part of the TBA identified earlier by Thibodeaux.

The process of bolivarization Hugo Chavez has been trying to establish is providing a network of characters that have been hostile to the USA government interests for decades. Chavez interest in advancing the "United States of Latin America," under his direct or indirect presidency, is easy to establish. He has proven a determination to engage the Latin American nations as a unit capable of competing for a superpower status under a century old proposal that failed over two centuries ago. He has nurtured the guerrilla groups in Latin America, and supported their initiatives and efforts against nations that maintain friendly relations with the USA. His government has been accused with evidence of using, at one point, petrodollars to interfere in the free electoral process throughout Latin America, using Miami, Florida as a transit point to deliver cash funds. The connection between narcotraffic and the bolivarization process has not been completed, as the subject of narcoterrorism will be presented next, leading to the USA's worst fears. The connection between the Russian Mafia, Latin American subversive groups, drug gangs, and cartels has surfaced at the time the USA is beginning to acknowledge our national security is under threat.

During the past few years Venezuela began a process of establishing transnational contacts that should have aroused suspicion. In 2008 I requested the presence of an expert on Venezuelan affairs to speak to my Advanced Placement Spanish class at the local high school. The class had conducted research on Latin American affairs, and was surprised at the connections Hugo Chavez had established. The Department of State considered several sources to speak to our students, but a few weeks before the event they decided to send Honorable Ambassador Patrick Duddy. Ambassador Duddy had been asked to leave Venezuela by President Hugo Chavez, and was gracious enough to speak to our students. A seasoned diplomat, he dodged the issue of Venezuela's global interference, and dismissed the political apparatus to appease the concerns our students had at that time. The fact is that our concern stemmed from several factors threatening the stability of the Western Hemisphere, specifically the USA's national security.

Hugo Chavez sought and received an agreement from the Soviet Union to provide weapons that include AK rifles; submarines; tanks; fighter jets; and the establishment of an ammunition factory. If we looked at a map of nations under security agreements with the Soviet Union, the whole world is under their security agreements except Australia, the USA, the European Union, and some countries in Western Africa. In 2008, the Russian Mafia groups were identified as linked to a global training group that has been established near the Mexican American border. The training camps include multinational agents representing Al Qaeda's Islamic Mayhreb, Hezbollah, Hamas, the FARC, and former government operatives under the former Soviet Union. This is known as the Foreign Terrorist Organization (Webster, 2008) which has been training gang cells for the Cartels under the Russian Mafia. These organizations are amassing their operations across the US – Mexican border in preparation for an impending attack. Even worst, trained operatives have received training and have been established in strategic locations throughout major rural cities in the USA. In addition to these activities (Webster, 2008), Mexico's National Migration Institute reported at the same time their concern with illegal immigrants from around the world entering the USA under disguise as Mexican citizens. This is in agreement and support of Carter's (Examiner, Jun 2010) report accusing Hugo Chavez of supporting multinational agent training in Cuba and Venezuela for the Mexican Ejercito Popular Revolucionario (Popular Revolutionary Army, PRA).

The cartels have advertised they are looking for "soldiers" to carry out their mandates enforcing their violent threats. Defectors from the Mexican and Guatemalan Army have joined the cartels for economic reasons. Training from the cartels includes weapons, tactics, and intelligence gathering. In the meantime, the DEA has been alerting of ghost planes flying several routes between Isla Margarita in Venezuela, South America, Central America, Europe, Western Africa, and Europe. These flights carry illegal drugs from the opium producing nations, and from the coke-cocaine countries. In 2008, a CIA operative expressed concern that the routes carried by these planes had become efficient at averting detection, which allowed for round-trips. The agent was concerned as to the type of cargo loaded into these planes returning to their point of origin.

A HAVEN FOR TERRORISM

There have been several reports issued by the United States on the Tri-Border Area and the speculation of terrorist activities in the region. On October 10, 2001, shortly after the September 11 terrorist attacks, "...the Department of State's coordinator for counter-terrorism told Congress that the TBA has the long-standing presence of Islamic extremist organizations, primarily Hezbollah" (Hudson 2003, p. 14). Other groups that are suspected of having a presence in the region are Al-Qaeda, Al-Jihad (Egyptian Islamic Jihad) and al-Muqawamah (Hudson, 2003, p. 12). Hezbollah has recently claimed a presence in Mexico, Venezuela, and other parts of Latin America.

Latin America has merged a cadre of presidents under the assumption that they will bring the antithesis of Perestroika to the USA. Presidents throughout the Western Hemisphere have formed an alliance with de juro and de facto actors from rouge terrorist supporting states that are either involved or support attacks against USA interests and/or American soil. The rhetoric involved has escalated into joint military exercises imitating USA efforts in the region. These activities, however, are open demonstrations from sworn governments responsible to the international community and organizations for their bellicose actions. The dilemma suffered by the people of Colombia, however, was the daily attacks suffered by a nation against an enemy that could not be held responsible for their actions. This historical experience has taught the narcoguerrillas a very valuable lesson that supports resilience, stubbornness, and determination. The modus operandi of these factions has brought training opportunities from around the world, weapons, supplies, and global support. Unexpectedly, these guerrillas have begun an apparent dismantling process, creating the false impression that the region will regain its quality of life. This attempt to project victory, nevertheless, may be the smokescreen covering Jihadists, terrorist supported organizations, and surprise assault attacks against USA soil. Concerns about narcoguerrillas cannot allow us to let our guard down with gang activity in the USA. The USA/DOJ's lawsuit against the state of Arizona has come at a time when law enforcement efforts must be backed by intense support from the National Guard troops posted on the USA border.

Colonel Curtis C. Connell, Commander of the Americas Division in the Office of the Deputy Undersecretary of Air Force International Affairs [states that] "terrorism just doesn't exist on the Islamic side, with a few minor exceptions" (Connell, 2006). Exceptions include Imad Mugniyah, Assad Ahmad Barakat, Sheik Mounir Fadel, and Salah Abdul Karim Yassine. "Lebanese commander of Hezbollah's overseas operations," Imad Mugniyeh, is said to have recruited the suicide bombers for the two terrorist attacks in the early 1990's in Argentina. He was originally the most wanted man by the United States until Osama Bin Laden replaced him with the September 11 attacks. Assad Ahmad Barakat, an accomplice of Mugniyeh and a Lebanese citizen of Ciudad Del Este played a crucial role in financing the bombing because he reportedly had a cell that made arrangements to import all the materials related to the attack into the TBA. In the years since then, investigators have identified Barakat as not only Hezbollah's military operations chief in the TBA, but also its chief Southern Cone fund-raiser (Hudson, 2003, p. 13).

It was also speculated by Argentinean courts that Barakat had made trips to Iran in 1990 and 1991, meeting with top Iranian officials, and then he traveled to Lebanon (Hudson, 2003, p. 14). Also identified by the Argentine security forces as a senior Hezbollah official is Sheik Mounir Fadel, "spiritual leader of Ciudad Del Este's main mosque" (Hudson, 2003, p. 16). In 2001, Fadel made several statements about the alleged ties of the Arab community to the terrorist organization. He stated that, "Hezbollah is a legitimate resistance group struggling against invaders into historically Arab lands" (Faiola, 2001). He also made the statement that, "local aid [raised in this region] goes solely to Hezbollah's humanitarian operations" (Ceaser, 2001). Just from this statement, it can be easy to come to the conclusion that there is a link between Hezbollah and this city in particular, although it is not a claim of direct support of terrorist activities by the organization. By 2003, as stated above, Fadel was suspected to be a senior Hezbollah official.

Several actors have been adding themselves to a larger list of individuals linked to organizations seeking the destruction of the USA. Salah Abdul Karim Yassine, a Palestinian suspected of offering his aid to Hamas, another Islamic terrorist organization, was found guilty in 2000 of being one of many terrorists involved in a plot to bomb U.S. and Israeli embassies in Asuncion. He was sentenced to four years in prison for illegal immigration and providing false documents (Hudson, 2003, p. 18-19). In February 2007, Zeaiter Rady Sohbi was arrested in Brazil. He had fake documents stating that he was a citizen of Paraguay. According to official reports, Sohbi was funneling profits from drug trafficking to Al-Qaeda accounts. He was originally in Ecuador but fled from police and ended up in Brazil ("Alleged Al-Qaida Financier Arrested in Brazil," 2007). The International Muslim Brotherhood has been associated with transnational banking transactions, known for money laundering profits from illegal narcotics trade.

The TBA is said to be an "ideal operations base for Arabic speaking terrorist or criminal groups." Because the community is so close and loyal to each other, it would be easy for a terrorist to commit a heinous crime and have an alibi prepared and supported by that community (Hudson, 2003, p. 9). As stated before, ninety percent of the Arab population in Ciudad Del Este and Foz de Iguazu are of Lebanese origin. The family origin of these Lebanese citizens traces to the Beka Valley in Lebanon, "which has been the epicenter of the Hezbollah organization" (Sverdlick, 2005, p. 85). Paraguayan police have charged several Paraguayan officials of allegedly selling illegal passports to foreigners traveling to Ciudad Del Este, including a few suspected terrorists (Faiola, 2001). One researcher from the area, however, states, "...the media has exaggerated the threat in relation to the Muslim communities of the region.... A large illicit community thrives in the area, but this does not necessarily mean that the Muslim community as a whole is involved" (Peres de Oliveira, 2006). It is outrageous to believe that the whole community supports terrorist activities; nevertheless, we can also argue that the community is responsible for the crime of omission and failure to report plots that include their incognito terrorist cells. This moral dilemma affiliates the Muslim community to the terrorist groups. Failure to report terrorist activity plotted by terrorist elements hiding behind religious groups create an unconditional allegiance between criminals and the community. Under criminal statutes, this is aiding and abetting criminals and criminal activity.

In late 2004, Al-Qaeda members were alleged to be recruiting members to carry out attacks on embassies of the United States, Britain, Spain and El Salvador throughout Latin America. Adnan G. El Shukrijumah is a terrorist suspect and was spotted in Honduras. Al-Qaeda was not specific in which countries the attacks were to be carried out. However, "governments throughout Mexico and Central America are on alert as evidence grows that Al-Qaeda members are traveling in the region and looking for recruits" ("Latin America on Alert for Terror," 2004). Connell's research on Islamist movements throughout Latin America indicates this group constitutes only about one percent (1%) of the Latin American population. They demand rights to exercise their religion. Ironically, their efforts to integrate their hosting communities to understand their religion are thwarted by their failure to translate material to be read in the target language. This creates an Islamic secluded and impenetrable community. Their location is strategic, and it is not coincidental that their relocation is in areas of corruption and lawlessness.

Here are several examples of alleged terrorist ties in the Triple Border Area and throughout Latin America. There is evidence that ties with Hezbollah as a political organization exist, but only alleged ties between the militant wing and this region. With so many alleged ties, perceptions of threats can go both ways. Either this is an attack on an Arab population, or the terrorists are working hard to cover their tracks. Was Sheik Mounir Fadel accused of being a terrorist because he announced his financial support for Hezbollah? He was a suspected senior Hezbollah official, but was it part of the militant or political wing of Hezbollah, or does the international community fails to distinguish a difference between the two? Hezbollah is a Lebanese political party with seats in the Lebanese government. But their militant wing is also a terrorist organization.

The analysis aimed at establishing the links and networks related to illegal drug traffic. A shift from illegal drug trade and the Bolivarization Movement led to a mudslide in which comprehension of the full process led us to the issue of narcoterrorism and its link to illegal drug trade. The most amazing component in this network is how Thibodeaux was able to lead the analysis from the Middle East into walking distance to the USA. The transition into the next chapter is necessary because we are still focused on the essential questions on whether drugs in the USA should be legalized or not. Looking deeper into the extent and roots associated to illegal drug trade will result in the right decision. Before closing, though, please keep in mind the following information. In Guatemala City the police have documented the existence of seventeen armed gangs associated with international drug dealers. The Guatemalan government currently holds 280 legal cases against legitimate arms dealers for selling weapons to drug traffickers. We also know that regional crime rings involving ex-combatants from both sides of the conflict have become involved in drug trafficking, kidnapping, extortion and bank assaults, especially in the area known as the Northern Triangle (Guatemala, Honduras, El Salvador and Nicaragua) Small arms are necessary to keep these enterprises going.

CHAPTER IV

NARCOTERRORISM AND BOLIVARIZATION:

Legalization's potential to diminish violence and criminality, and...the control of nuclear proliferation in the Western Hemisphere?

The following assertions have been addressed by Thibodeaux, yet merit reinforcement. The Colombian phenomenon responsible for national and transcontinental criminality suddenly has established itself across our border. The government of the Estados Unidos de Mexico reported nearly 30,000 drug related gruesome murders and crimes have been committed between 2006 and 2010, which include mass graves. Decapitations and drive-by shootings along the Mexican-American border adversely affect the quality of life in Mexico, as well as along the bordering states in the USA. The response to the disruption in our daily routine has tilted all the extremes. California attempted to pass a law legalizing marijuana, while Arizona attempted to parallel federal laws holding the illegal immigrant community accountable to the judicial system. Both measures have prompted protests and criticism from most Latin American countries against the USA's government.

Latin America has merged a cadre of presidents under the assumption that they will bring the antithesis of Perestroika to the USA. Presidents throughout the Western Hemisphere have formed an alliance with de juro and de facto actors from rouge terrorist supporting states that are either involved or support attacks against USA interests and/or American soil. The rhetoric involved has escalated into joint military exercises imitating USA efforts in the region. These activities, however, are open demonstrations from sworn governments responsible to the international community and organizations for their bellicose actions. The dilemma suffered by the people of Colombia, however, was the daily attacks suffered by a nation against an enemy that could not be held responsible for their actions. This historical experience has taught the narcoguerrillas a very valuable lesson that supports resilience, stubbornness, and determination. The modus operandi of these factions has brought training opportunities from around the world, weapons, supplies, and global support. Unexpectedly, these guerrillas have begun an apparent dismantling process, creating the false impression that the region will regain its quality of life. This attempt to project victory, nevertheless, may be the smokescreen covering Jihadists, terrorist supported organizations, and surprise assault attacks against USA soil. Concerns about narcoguerrillas cannot allow us to let our guard down with gang activity in the USA. The USA/DOJ's lawsuit against the state of Arizona has come at a time when law enforcement efforts must be backed by intense support from the National Guard troops posted on the USA border.

Thibodeaux cautiously begins this segment sharing her expertise by establishing terrorist links to the TBA. In March 1992, the Israeli Embassy in Argentina was bombed by a suicide bomber, which killed 29 people and wounded 135 others. The case has remained unsolved (McDonnell, 2006). Originally, a group known as 'Pro-Palestine,' and later the group known as Islamic Jihad, claimed responsibility for the attacks, but there was no confirmation of who was responsible ("Argentina Asks Interpol to Arrest Hezbollah Leader," 2002). "Just previously to the embassy bombing, the Israelis were in southern Lebanon. They killed the military commander of Hezbollah" (Connell, 2006). Because of the large Arab population in this region between the three countries, this attack on the Israeli Embassy could be seen as retaliation by Lebanese supporters.

Two years later, in July 1994, it was speculated that a suicide bomber for Hezbollah was responsible for the detonation of a van outside the Argentina Israelite Mutual Association in Buenos Aires (McDonnell, 2006). It was suggested that "Iran's top leaders were motivated to order the bombing by Argentina's decision in 1992 to cut off its supply of nuclear materials to Iran." However, Argentina and Iran were still having negotiations over the issue when both the bombings happened (Porter, 2006). Moshen Rabbani, the Iranian Embassy attaché in Argentina, was accused by officials in the Argentinean government of "having provided logistical assistance to Hezbollah elements that entered Argentina illegally" through the Tri-Border Area to carry out the 1994 bombing ("Argentina Asks Interpol to Arrest Hezbollah Leader," 2002). This is just one of several examples of alleged ties between the TBA and terrorist organizations.

The TBA where Brazil, Argentina, and Paraguay meet is a region suffering from money laundering, narcotics trafficking, and piracy of computer software and music (Sverdlick, 2005, p.88). The three cities involved heavily in these illegal activities are Ciudad Del Este (Paraguay), Foz de Iguazu (Brazil) and Puerto Iguazu in Argentina. Ciudad Del Este is Paraguay's second largest city. "Arabic is heard as much as, or perhaps more than, Spanish" in this city (Hudson, 2003, p. 6-8). Ciudad Del Este is an alleged safe-haven for Islamic terrorists, and "a major transshipment point for drugs, not to mention a center of black market commerce" (Pion-Berlin, 2000, p. 56). The Pan American Highway runs through this city connecting it to Curitiba, Brazil. Foz de Iguazu is Brazil's most violent city, having 180 homicides in 2000 and 275 homicides in 2002. Ninety percent of the Arab population (with a rough estimate of 30,000 people) in Ciudad Del Este and Foz de Iguazu is Lebanese (Hudson, 2003, p. 8). Puerto Iguazu, Argentina does not have any Arab or Jewish communities (Sverdlick, 2005, p. 85).

Although the issues of drug trafficking, corruption and money laundering do not have a direct impact on the United States security in the way that terrorism has, and could possibly be handled by the three countries involved, the presence of a Lebanese population in this region raises alarm with the countries fighting in the War on Terrorism, particularly the United States. A major issue is whether the United States is discriminating against this region by targeting it simply because of its Arab population, or whether there is enough evidence to support the claim that Hezbollah, a Lebanese organization whose militant wing conducts terrorist activities throughout the world and is supported by the Iranian regime, conducts financing operations and/or terrorist operations in this area (Byman, 2003). The operations that need to be examined are whether they have an operating base in this area, and whether they are receiving funds from the illegal activities such as money laundering and narcotics trafficking. Also analyzed is the effect MERCOSUR, the Common Market of the South, has on the illegal activities that affect the region on the borders of these three countries.

NARCOTRAFFICK, MONEY LAUNDERING, CORRUPTION: FUNDING TERRORISM

Money laundering, corruption and narcotics trafficking are interrelated. The National Anti-Drug Secretariat of Paraguay suggests that "narcotics trafficking generates approximately 40% of the laundered funds" in the region. It is also suggested that the officials who are responsible for combating corruption are the same ones that are facilitating money laundering (Sverdlick, 2005, p. 88). Ignoring corrupt states is at the peril of the international community. Corrupt states are "...incubators of terrorism, the narcotics trade, money laundering, human trafficking, and other global crime- raising issues far beyond corruption" (Heimann and Heineman, 2006). Corrupt officials and politicians have "used the black market to transmit their illegally obtained wealth" (Brazilian Politician Charged with Theft of Over 11 Million Dollars," 2007).

It is estimated that between US$300 million and US$500 million in profits is sent from the TBA every year from fundamentalist groups in this area to Islamic groups in the Middle East. These profits come from "drug trafficking, arms dealing, and other illegal activities including money-laundering, human trafficking, contraband, and product piracy" (Hudson, 2003, p. 4). The profits are easily transferred, "with lax border controls and more than 100 hidden airstrips in the region" (Hudson, 2003, p. 24). "There are no controls on the amount of currency that can be brought into or out of the country, and there are no cross border reporting requirements. Little in the way of personal background information is required to open a bank account or to make financial transactions in Paraguay; therefore, there is a high incidence of money-laundering activities" (Hudson, 2003, p. 53).

Approximately 18 of 42 identified terrorist organizations across the globe are, "involved in some aspect of drug trafficking activity to fund their operations." Some terrorist organizations collect money through taxes while other groups are involved "in virtually every aspect of drug trafficking activity" (Green, 2006). Hezbollah drug factories "produce an estimated 60 to 70 percent of the final product which they proceed to sell at a prodigious profit. Much of these ill-gotten gains are funneled through the TBA" (Thomson, 2006). Businesses that are used to launder the money often ship large sums of money overseas, but "do not pay income taxes for two or three years because of a lack of income." It is suspected that terrorists are using these businesses to launder the money and ultimately fund the terrorist activities (Sverdlick, 2005, p. 88).

Assad Ahmad Barakat supposedly was involved in money laundering that helped finance Al-Qaeda operations. He was owner of Mondial Engineering and Construction, money laundering front company with offices in Beirut and Ciudad Del Este. It was suspected that the money made from real estate fraud by this company was funneled to Al- Qaeda. A Lebanese citizen, Ali Assi, was caught with ten kilos of cocaine at the Beirut airport in 2002. Assi happens to be the owner of a coffee shop in Ciudad Del Este, as well as the father-in-law of Ali Hassan Abdallah, who worked along side Barakat as the coordinator of the TBA's Hezbollah financial network (Hudson, 2003, p. 25). Here is Barakat, a suspected recruiter for Hezbollah, Assi, who is smuggling drugs, and Abdallah, the connection between the two. It is possible, with this connection, that Abdallah is involved in both the drug trafficking and terrorist operations.

COMBATING TERRORISM IN THE TRI-BORDER AREA AND IN LATIN AMERICA: ILLEGAL FINANCIAL ACTIVITIES THAT FUND TERRORIST ORGANIZATIONS

From an international perspective, it is important to analyze the situation in this region because there is a potential terrorist threat. It is reported that "as many as 10 million illegal immigrants may have entered the United States last year [2005]" (Mittelstadt, 2006). Roughly 46% of the people arrested for illegal immigration from Mexico come from Brazil ("Latin America on Alert for Terror," 2004). Drug cartels have smuggling routes across the U.S.-Mexico border, using these routes for human smuggling and narcotics trafficking. For a fee, those that specialize in human smuggling could transport terrorists across the border (Gamboa, 2006). It was reported in 2003 that a group of Mexican "coyotes," or human smugglers, transported a group of Muslims into the USA. Once they crossed the border they stopped to call their contacts in North Carolina. Apparently, funding for their trip was available through this contact. According to Wagner (2007), the Muslim American Brotherhood (MAS), a branch of the International Muslim Brotherhood, the terrorist networks established in the USA aim at gathering funding for their attacks.

The Mexican cartels turf war in 2010 create concern and fear that we may be facing more than a war on drugs across the Rio Grande.

Terrorists can make their way through the Gulf Coast of Mexico, or they can make their way up from the Tri-Border Area to the Mexican border. The Mexican navy was supposed to have stepped up security on the coast line to hinder any terrorist plots on its oil supply. Al-Qaeda leaders had called for an attack on Mexico's oil supply to hurt the U.S. economy. This would force the USA to increase its dependence on Venezuelan oil. One news agency said one of its reporters approached the oil fields with ease and no questions were asked, and then concluded that a terrorist could infiltrate the area easily (Hall, 2007). If terrorists are able to obtain Venezuelan passports which facilitate the crossing of interstate borders, then it is imperative for every state to focus much of its security on the people traveling across borders as well as areas on the state borders that lack effective controls. In Paraguay, it is estimated that only one out of every twenty border crossers are checked for passports. At one location there may be several law enforcement officials, but just a few miles up the road the traffickers cross the borders using boats (Reel, 2006).

"Brazil, Paraguay and Argentina have agreed to set up a joint intelligence center in the Brazilian border town of Foz de Iguazu to clamp down on smuggling, drug-trafficking and money laundering in the Triple Border Area" ("MERCOSUR: New intelligence force to operate in TBA," 2006). By improving law enforcement and eradicating criminal activities, these three countries could reduce any threat of terrorism in this region (Connell, 2006). "On May 31, 1996,the three TBA nations established a "Tripartite Command of the Tri-Border" in an effort to better control commerce and the large transient international population" (Hudson, 2003, p. 60). It is likely that any efforts to provide support to control criminal activities in Latin America will provide the USA with improvements in our national security.

MERCOSUR

MERCOSUR is the Common Market of the South and involves South American countries members that include Brazil, Argentina, Uruguay and Paraguay; plus associate members include Chile, Colombia, Ecuador, Peru and Bolivia; with Venezuela becoming its newest member in 2006 ("Update 1-Roundup," 2006). In the early 1970s, when Brazil and Paraguay were seeking to exploit the energy generating and tourist potential of Iguassú Falls and to promote regional trade, government planners established a free-trade zone in the rapidly growing boomtown city of Ciudad del Este, thereby allowing Argentines and Brazilians to purchase cheap electronic products there. The TBA, with already more than half a million inhabitants, soon became a lawless jungle corner of Argentina, Brazil, and Paraguay (Hudson, 2003).

"The creation of MERCOSUR has meant the lowering of trade to the free flow of goods between the member countries…" (Pion-Berlin, 2000: 43). It is important that, even though the economic barriers on goods has been lowered, security needs to be tightened. "While MERCOSUR encourages the free flow of goods across borders, Paraguay's black marketers and criminals exploit that freedom, thereby cutting into MERCOSUR's gains from normal commercial relations" (Pion-Berlin, 2000, p. 56). With effective border patrol, these three countries might be able to hinder any kind of illegal movement of goods throughout this region as well as throughout the countries involved. "Part of the rationale for setting up a Southern Cone defense system would be to confront an array of illegal border transgressions, including narcotrafficking, terrorism, and immigration" (Pion-Berlin, 2000, p. 53). Paraguay is refusing to allow its military to be involved in fighting narcotics trafficking, and this could be because of the higher rate of involvement of military officials in narcotics trafficking (Pion-Berlin, 2000, p. 56). If these officials were allowed to control border crossings, they might accept bribes from traffickers which would undermine what MERCOSUR is trying to achieve. Although Paraguay does not produce much domestically, and therefore offers little to MERCOSUR trade, it is vital for Paraguay to stay in the market, because it is probable that the country "would rely exclusively on the underground market" if it cancels its membership with MERCOSUR (Pion-Berlin, 2000, p. 56). This would have a negative effect on the region and on the attempt to integrate the countries of Latin America. It has been proven that international integration greatly reduces national corruption. "Countries that are more integrated into international society are more exposed to economic and normative pressures against corruption…" (Grey and Sandholt 2003: 761). On the other hand, limiting the power of the military to intervene in the free transit of illegal drugs contributes to the corruption and lawlessness process that nurtures the establishment of Hezbollah and other terrorist groups in the TBA.

MERCOSUR states were originally negotiating with Israel on a trade treaty before the summer 2006 war between Lebanon and Israel. There has been tension since that war because Brazil supported Lebanon after several of its citizens were killed by Israeli forces. Brazil's government also states that Hezbollah is not a terrorist organization. It is a recognized legitimate political organization in Lebanon that also happens to conduct terrorist operations. As a result, Brazil had backed out of negotiations for this reason among others, but Argentina was still pushing for the trade treaty ("Brazil Puts MERCOSUR-Israel Free Trade Agreement on Back Burner," 2006). It is important for the security of the region and for each country in particular that MERCOSUR flourishes. This will combine forces against any evils they are confronted with, and it will help their economy. Failure to address the fact that the TBA area is considered a transit zone for illegal drugs also helps the underground economy that, according to experts, cushioned illegal drug producing nations from the severe economic fallout in the first decade of the twenty-first century.

NARCOTERRORISM THROUGHOUT THE WESTERN HEMISPHERE: INTERFERENCE WITH NATIONAL SECURITY

Thibodeaux's analysis is specifically aimed at the TBA region, establishing how Hezbollah and Islamic fundamentalist groups utilize illegal drug trade profit to fund terrorist organizations. Venezuela's connection with narco-guerrillas has been reported through the news media for almost a decade, yet diplomacy and international politics has been incapable of deterring Hugo Chavez' efforts to destabilize the region. Reports throughout the world indicate the black market selling fraudulent passports enables terrorist cells to enter any nation (Greenberg, 2007). Chavez decrease of requirements to obtain passports in Venezuela opened a door to provide legal international entrance to any element seeking a passport from Venezuela, prompting some nations to reject traveler's entrance to some countries if their passports indicate certain irregularities.

Under the Bolivarian War, Venezuela has relaxed many international laws to invite subversive group cooperation with the hemispheric network he has established. We have already connected Venezuela to the narcoguerrillas in Colombia. It is also public domain information that Chavez' network includes Iran, North Korea, Russia, and China. Contrary to our initial intention to provide recognition between narcotic trade and terrorism, it became evident that the apparent silence from terrorist groups since 9/11 is based on the possibility of an impending catastrophic event or series of events in the USA. Thibodeaux and I have been able to identify the global narcoterrorist network from published work, but we had agreed a major actor threatening our national security had been avoiding recognition behind the Middle East sleeper cells.

While working in Colombia in 2002, some nuclear material used to detect oil deposits disappeared, creating concern among all the national security agencies. This material was recovered, along with recognition that rural, mountainous, and jungle regions in the country could host unrecognized and undetected enemies. Kuna Indians from the Panamanian Archipelago, an isolated zone, confided their concerns with guerrilla groups traveling through Kuna Islands and the Darien zone. According to the Kuna's, the Colombian guerrillas make incursions to their islands undetected by the Panamanian government. Efforts by the Panamanian government to stop the transit of guerrilla groups through the Darien Zone have also been ineffective. The question to ask is why the guerrilla groups are traveling to the north through Panama.

The Kuna Indians enjoyed one of the most peaceful societies in the Western Hemisphere for over 93 years. The guerrilla's home invasions included stealing and subjecting the Kuna's to instability created by the uncertainty of suffering death threats typical of the FARC and ELN. Our concern at that time, 1993, was the possibility these guerrillas could control passage through the Panama Canal. Maintaining some bases in the Canal Zone seemed to be a permanent possibility after returning the Canal Zone to the government of Panama, along with keeping the anti-narcotic operations base in the Canal Zone. The unexpected move in the 1990's to prevent USA interests in all these operations, along with granting the Panama's Port Authority operations contract to the Hutchinson-Whampoon shipping company, seemed unreasonable but not an actual threat to our national security. Chinese control of railroad and canal operations do raise actual concerns due to the fact that according to Eland (1999) the company's affiliation has been linked to China's People Liberation Army and their intelligence services.

Within the last five years Venezuela has also contracted agreements with the government of China to provide over 3,500 technical advisors. The Chinese advisors will provide expertise to develop oil deposits in several regions in Venezuela, providing China with unlimited supplies of oil. United States purchase of oil from Venezuela will suffer significant increases if China becomes the main oil buyer. Since 1999 we have seen an increase in the Chinese presence in the Western Hemisphere. Technical advisors have settled in Panama to support government operations through the Canal, plus control of the railroad system that supports the movement of diversified global transaction elements with several continents through the Panama Canal Zone. Hugo Chavez' request for technical assistance compounds with the Chinese presence north of Colombia. The red flags associated to this assistance are not an overreaction; instead an expansion beyond Venezuelan soil into the Continental USA.

In previous chapters we also mentioned the Honduran connection with Chinese citizens; know as "el chinazo." Chinese nationals entered Honduras and purchased from the government Honduran citizenship. In addition, the government also provided these Chinese citizens passports to enter the USA legally as Honduran citizens. The quantity of Chinese immigrants entering the USA through this method does not serve justice when compared to Asian – Pacific Islanders entering the USA through human trafficking avenues. Aside from the Chinese connection to Honduras, the large Islamic colony in Honduras is a subject of interest for us. Reports of visitors from the Italian Mafia in the region, along with concerns about the nuclear traveling suitcases, are nothing less than added fuel to an existing fire.

The worst case scenario with the China connection would be unrelated to illegal immigrants and technical advisors. The emerging threat is the training available to subversive groups throughout Latin America, and their threat to the sovereign status of every nation in the Western Hemisphere. Technical advisors from China provided the expertise to engage in the social cleansing process throughout Cambodia, Laos and Viet Nam. Groups called "liberation Army" and "national Army" swept through rural areas in Southeast Asia to force their economic and political system. Support from the government of China enabled the Khmer Rouge troops to impose terror and fear throughout the region, forcing the silence of government opponents. Fields of massacred villagers under the hands of the "liberation army" and "national army" are documented history in the region. It took years for reports of these massacres to become available for the Western civilizations to become aware of the brutal regimes imposed with China's support. The new militias in Venezuela have been approved by Chavez to carry weapons at all times, creating concern as to the objective behind arming his loyal militias.

The fact that Venezuela, Honduras, and Panama have a substantial presence of Chinese nationals affiliated to the People's Republic of China commands attention at the type of training available to subversive and revolutionary groups south of the USA border. The ruthlessness of Latin American guerrillas is nothing in comparison to the mercenary violence linked to the Golden Triad and the Chinese opium gangs. One can only imagine the fate of the Western Hemisphere if the drug cartel narcoguerrillas joined forces with Chinese drug gangs. The violence against the Latin American population would rise to intimidating levels.

The government of Peru has suffered indigenous uprisings against their government. President Alan Garcia of Peru faced an early setback in 2010, as law enforcement officers were murdered by radical opponents supported by the Venezuelan government of dictator Hugo Chavez. President Garcia has engaged Peru in an outstanding economic and societal development process to provide core emerging opportunities throughout the Andean region. Chavez support for President Garcia's government subsidized and encouraged Alberto Pizango's indigenous uprising against the democratically elected government of President Garcia. Garcia's initiatives have also brought agreements to control public and government corruption. Undermining these initiatives, and prompting an underground terrorist movement, Pizango led radical opponents linked to the Shinning Path Guerrillas (Movimiento Sendero Luminoso) and the Tupac Amaru Revolutionary Movement to block the Belaunde Terry Highway, depriving regions that depend on this route for needed food, energy, and medicine in addition to disrupting trade. Chavez support for Pizango has brought a merging between radical proponents of indigenous rights which in turn oppose a free market system.

The tactics used by Pizango, however, are not typical of the behavior characteristic of indigenous groups. Having traveled through the Andean region, it is obvious that the tribes have been trapped into waves of radical groups swaying their loyalty to advance an agenda that maintains the indigenous labor force in a permanent status of economic deprivation. The incident in Peru is representative of an upsurge in violent behavior that has led the community representation as bizarre and violent. The incident referred to last year engaged a group of law enforcement officers, unarmed, with indigenous rebels blocking a highway. The officer's assignment required clearing the population from the main highway to open the transit route to the public, which had been blocked over a month, led by Pizango. The result of unarmed officers assigned to this task was 33 deaths, including among them twenty four police officers who had their throats cut. It is unlikely that the members of the tribes would have engaged in such violence without assistance from subversive groups. It is of national opinion that the indigenous tribes were misled, as one report indicates that assemblies before the blockade included remarks from instigators demanding violent acts to force the government into complying with their mandates. These patterns of sedition and insurrection are not geared to accomplish what is best for the nation, but instead fulfill a hidden agenda.

The indigenous people of Peru have been receiving assistance from Hugo Chavez' Bolivarian Alternative for the Americas' Homes (ALBA), which provide medical assistance throughout the area. The government of President Garcia has raised concerns that the social programs established through the Bolivarian Movement are serving to indoctrinate uneducated groups throughout Latin America. However, USA assistance has been declined by many countries out of fear of interference from the Venezuelan government, increasing the level of intimidation and threats projected by the Venezuelan government. In 2002 many Colombians were concerned that the government of Fidel Castro was providing medical school scholarships throughout the Western Hemisphere to indigent students. Their concern was that these groups of adolescents would be alienated and indoctrinated into Marxist and Maoist doctrines, in exchange for a profession. Their return to their country would require serving rural communities that suffer from a lack of medical services. Insurrections from indigenous groups, precisely from areas of difficult access, indicate there is some type of motivation and organized efforts probably instigated under the leadership of well trained individuals to disrupt national security. The slaughter of these policemen has not been brought up to justice. Pizango was granted asylum in Managua, Nicaragua where he has spent the first half of the year 2010.

Iran's largest embassy in the Western Hemisphere is also located in Nicaragua. Although the Iranian community in Nicaragua is not that large, the destination of a daily flight from Managua to Caracas is Tehran. President Daniel Ortega from Nicaragua has agreed to allow Iran to build a deep-sea port, 10,000 homes, and electric plants in his country. However, the islanders have expressed their displeasure at building such port, interfering with their natural environment and quality of life. A dry canal would be built, as planned, between Monkey Port Bay accessing the Gulf of Mexico, and the Port of Corinto accessing the Pacific Ocean. Concern in the region has risen since twenty one elite guard Iranians have entered the country "undercover" (Bensman 2008) in addition to engaging in more traveling in the region. The Al-Quds, Iran's elite revolutionary guard, have also been engaged in strengthening the Venezuelan secret service and police (Fleischman 2009). Their presence throughout Latin America raises questions about the role of the elite guard in the Western Hemisphere. We speculate their role in Nicaragua involves the establishment of training camps.

Other reports from the Wall Street Journal (2009) offer a very interesting perspective of Iranian financial investments around Africa, Central and South America. Factories and banks have been opened, are operational, and maintain employees; however, the products and customers are not visible. A car factory in Venezuela, for example, produces non-profit cars for social redistribution. However, the cars cannot be sold to the public; they are only for government use. Other Iranian investments in Africa, for example, have failed short of production even though the factories continue regular operations. This lack of material evidence from functional enterprises may be representative of a new international investment trend to launder profits from illegal ventures. It may also represent shell industries used to export and import materials under embargo and/or nuclear enrichment transactions aimed at creating nuclear states in the Western Hemisphere. Training from tyrannical regimes to unstable democracies is a worrisome initiative, especially if indigenous forces are being recruited to engage on violent acts typical of terrorist groups.

Venezuela's interference in Peru using Bolivarian operatives forces recognition that Chavez intentions to establish the "Bolivarian Republic" will become a reality either through quasi democratic elections or by force. The modus operandi in Peru's attack against law enforcement officers sets a precedent. The guerrilla warfare tactics merger with fundamentalist Islamic terrorist groups will present a challenge of major proportions in the most unusual asymmetric war in the twenty-first century. Fleischman's assertion that Latin America will be facing totalitarian rule is a realistic probability, especially if we are talking about unexpected sanguinary suicidal tactics. The element of surprise will be a fundamental factor to recognize in an effort to prevent and avoid an emerging hemispheric terrorist guerrilla war.

Revising the Colombian incident with limited nuclear material, one could rightfully conclude that offers from Venezuela and Bolivia to provide uranium to Iran must be reciprocated with an offer to share the uranium enrichment process. Faithful flights from Nicaragua, Caracas, Damascus, and Tehran are reportedly used to transport missile materials. Accordingly, high ranking military officials, high ranking intelligence officers, and troops traveling without visas may be part of the passengers entering Latin America from Iran. Likewise, a transshipment of supposedly tractor parts was confiscated, exposing the Venezuelan cargo from Iran as not tractor parts but weapon components. Investigations are still in place to determine the possibility these could also be linked link to radioactive material. A look at the variety of enterprises associated to current business transactions between Iran and Latin America, we could rightfully conclude Iran's interest in the region is creeping into Central and South America, with a likely focus on the USA. This rules out an Iranian development trade partnership using diplomatic relations, and brings in enough questions about Iran's interest in racing to establish the grounds needed towards an underground movement geared to promote insurrection in this hemisphere.

This underground insurrection, as we have recognized previously, has been supported by funding from illegal drug trade. It forces voters to weight the pros and cons of legalizing drugs. Dr. W. Kilmer had suggested writing a manual as my project in 1996, which prompted an unconditional "no" at the time, as I could not engage my personal ethics into even contemplating legalization as a remote possibility. The approach from Dr. R. Thompson helped me share the initiatives implemented in Colombia in 2002. A study of the decrease in violence in Colombia from 2002 until the spring of 2010 shows the use of a similar approach in Colombia has provided positive results. Today's headlines indicate the Colombian narcoguerrillas suffered another important loss, the death of Mono JoJoy. Campground location and internal information was provided to military groups, resulting on a very effective attack against the FARC. We had been contemplating the truth behind assertions that the narcoguerrillas could replace the cartels. The Colombian government of Jose Manuel Santos, Uribe's replacement, retaliated against the FARC's threats with evidence of his intentions. The lack of rhetoric from President Santos makes him a man of few words but effective actions. He began his presidency after Uribe successfully laid the ground for an attempt to bring peace in Colombia. The fall of 2010 has brought speculation on the fate of the Colombian cartels and guerrillas.

FROM NARCOTERRORISM TO GANGRILLAS: USA 2011?

The fax phone was ringing at 10:30 pm when we walked into our home an April evening in 2010. I knew it had to be one of our kids, as no one else has our fax number except business contacts. It had been over seven years since I had heard the voice at the other end, and my first instinct was to hang up, but I knew this had to deal with our national security. If this sounds like an old love affair, trust me the caller at the other end could have been my child, and our contacts had been strictly professional. It also reminded me of our uncanny experiences in Colombia. After 9/11, I felt there was a need to investigate the possibility that guerrilla groups in Colombia could be engaged in the acquisition of nuclear weapons. This thought had crossed my mind while I completed my graduate project addressing the problem of illegal drugs in Latin America. There were many nights I had anxiety attacks imagining the world of possibilities associated to narcotraffic. One of the reasons I accepted to work the *Unicurrículo Colombiano* for Plan Colombia was because Ray Rivera (ICITAP 2002) called me as part of a team that "could land running." He had tried for four years to complete the project but continued to put it on hold because of matters we did not discuss. Taking the job would lead me close to the Colombian people and would help me get an idea of which route I would take. The FBI had already granted my security clearance, which was unnecessary, as everything we faced was published in the Colombian newspapers before we were aware. It would be a lie to tell you that this was one of the regular jobs we had completed throughout Latin America.

Completing the curriculum was a first step, followed by setting up a pilot course to present the program and validate its effectiveness. We would continue providing training until several steps had been completed. This process would provide the Colombians with a source available throughout all of Latin America. Lou, Raul, and I would be working as a team traveling until the process was completed. Ray worked with us and later was replaced with Mike until some directors were hired at high levels. Both were excellent seasoned administrators, facilitating each step of the process. After we completed the curriculum and began the pilot course, the ICITAP administrator at the time I refer to as Miss Missy was placed in charge of ICITAP Colombia and suddenly our support group to continue working with the Colombians vanished. As soon as we began the Pilot Course Ms. Missy hired a team from Texas, and all the work we had completed was credited to other consultants. We cried with anger at the lack of understanding shown by ICITAP Colombia, jeopardizing the efforts to unite the Colombian agencies. Even worst, it was clear that the US military teams proved their efficiency at recognizing the internal strife in the country and looking beyond and above to stabilize the country. The strategic military process planning and relying on using data to achieve effective results must be mirrored by other departments in the USA engaged in intelligence gathering. It was clear that part of the problem completing the **Unicurriculo** was some federal agencies failure to understand the mission of the DEA in the war on drugs. Except for the military's focus, and the DEA's ability to continue the war on drugs, ICITAP Colombia failed to understand their efforts had to be orchestrated with the mission.

There are no details included in this book causing any federal or state agency to believe our national security has been exposed. The data and facts covered come from reports and news available through the internet and academic published materials, except for a handful of venting incidents. Knowledge obtained while completing my Masters in Latin America and the problems with narcotics, and Thibodeaux's outstanding research on the Middle East and the TBA helped us organize these events and identify specific operations aimed at destabilizing the national security of the USA. We're still providing you with the facts that will help you determine how the narcotic's trade network is of such complexity that the decision to legalize drugs in the USA is not based on only a level of criminality or violence. You must take the following facts under consideration, as well as how all the federal, state, and local law enforcement agencies have been operating to control illegal drugs, while at the same time an agenda of greater magnitude runs an underground current capable of destabilizing the national security of the USA.

Nuclear material has been reported in other segments of the book as used to determine the underground petroleum availability in petroleum producing countries. Such material, used in Colombia, disappeared from a test site. A search was conducted, failing to provide the investigative team with the proper equipment to prevent toxic nuclear contamination, failing to protect first responders. After becoming aware of this situation, we took a look at several South American nations testing for oil deposits. The main nation is Venezuela, under the direction of Hugo Chavez. During the last seven years, we have kept informed on Venezuela's progress.

The news has reports of Hugo Chavez in Cuba, and the connections he provided to the guerrilla groups in Colombia, Mexico, and throughout Latin America. Chavez has also traveled to Russia, North Korea, Iran, and China. Connections in each of these countries are clear, and have been publicly identified to some extent. We have also been able to establish the movements throughout Latin America that aim at undermining the national stability in the USA. These efforts have not created any concern among the American citizens. The post 9/11 crisis created a thicker survival core among Americans in the USA, while its smokescreen covered the preparation process for the next attack. Sadam Hussein's statements threatened the destruction of the USA from the ground up. During almost a decade in Iraq and Afghanistan, this threat has not materialized overseas as promised. We have failed to look under our own ground for movements leading to materialize this threat.

In Guatemala City the police have documented the existence of seventeen armed gangs associated with international drug dealers. The Guatemalan government currently holds 280 legal cases against legitimate arms dealers for selling weapons to drug traffickers. We also know that regional crime rings involving ex-combatants from both sides of the civil unrest conflict have become involved in drug trafficking, kidnapping, extortion and bank assaults, especially in the area known as the Northern Triangle (Guatemala, Honduras, El Salvador and Nicaragua) Small arms are necessary to keep these enterprises going, and Venezuela has made it clear it has been preparing for an attack against its enemy: the USA.

Gangs have sprouted throughout Latin America, many of them with the remnants of disengaged revolutionary groups that lost their fertile ground during the decade of the 1990's, and the first decade of this millennium. Their basis moved into providing transportation, security, and distribution for cartels and illegal drug dealers. We have spoken about how the DEA's success always led the cartels to create innovative ways to overcome federal anti-narcotic setbacks. In addition, we have also experienced decades of successful measures that were immediately overturned with an increase in activity, indicating our federal agencies efforts had been fruitless. We clearly stated that, instead of identifying these as failures, we needed to recognize how the joint efforts from the DEA, Department of Defense, FBI, and our intelligence gathering community completed their mission to find out their efforts launched improvements in refining criminality among ruthless foreigners.

We are beginning the second decade of the new millennium facing a war against a new breed of terrorists capable of destroying our rural and urban infrastructure. Evidence that the DEA efforts succeeded in Latin America were published on October 2010 after the FARC lost its second man in command. The unified federal law enforcement and military efforts in Latin America destroyed the fragile infrastructure of the Colombian narcoguerrillas. Rest assured, however, that our sigh of relief will be marked with frantic measures when we recognize the narcoguerrillas have been granted a new global mission. The illegal drug traffic guerrillas have been providing training, and will unleash a new breed of illegal mutant gangs and guerrillas to be known as **Gangrillas.**

Rural and urban areas are experiencing graffiti indicators that gangs have established themselves in the area. The graffiti involves enemy groups fighting their turf war. Recruitment of these members is eerie at best, as young people are becoming disengaged from their families in behalf of membership in these groups. These trends are actually a modernized version of the distinct process suffered in Colombia two decades ago. Madam Hillary Clinton's assertion in September 2010 that Mexico is showing signs of evolving into a narco state, similar to Colombia twenty years ago is of great significance. In addition, she is alerting the Council on Foreign Relations that Mexico's problems with the cartel shows signs of an insurgency in the country.

In June 2010, Congressman Sue Myrick (R – NC) requested information from the Department of Homeland Security (DHS) about the link between Hezbollah and the Mexican Cartels. Her request was aligned with diverse reports that Hezbollah operatives had established connections with Colombian drug cartels. During the same time period, Hezbollah was linked to an illegal drug smuggling network transporting cocaine and opium derivatives to/from Colombia to Europe through Gambia, Africa. Purchases of Scud missiles from Syria allowed Hezbollah to situate these aimed at Israeli soil. Congressman Myrick's concern was voiced, however, when a car bomb exploded near the Mexico – USA border. Myrick's concern reflects worries generated among the intelligence community, which indicate drug smuggling and human trafficking through our bordering states probably also include terrorist cells subsidized by illegal drug traffic. Her direct approach to DHS Director Janet Napolitano surfaced when the so called "Mexican Cartels" were accused of exploding a car bomb, which is an Eastern terrorist group tactic. It is ironic to think funding generated by American's dependency on illegal drugs, and our failure to address the root of the problem that leads to addiction, will drive our nation into unleashed violence of unimagined proportions.

This violence is at an incubator stage, setting up very cautiously the ground to a threatening level of massive criminality in the USA. Madame Clinton's concerns and Congressman Myrick both lack an element of information missing on these issues that are about to become reality. In 2009 we were informed that gangs had targeted juveniles in the school systems. These gang leaders made sure the secondary school system was not aware of who these individuals were within the community of educators or law enforcement. An increase in disruptions and harassment from these individuals cannot be linked to gangs, causing the system to confront gang activity that cannot be linked to the judicial system's effort to control and disrupt these organized criminal groups. Their actions also deprive the educational community from addressing illegal drug activity in the school systems as part of criminal organizations, making them look as isolated cases of personal drug addiction and personal possession. Unrecognized new trends are engaging young adolescents in a network of activities that deteriorate the support network of children and their families. The nuclear family structure, especially at times of economic disadvantage, may exhibit a developing trend slowly leading high school groups of students to promote sexual abuses against young females, at the same time that the gay community rights are violated. Very subtle activity indicates Hispanic young people are lured into prostitution as well as human and drug trafficking.

The countries of Venezuela and the Iranian Islamic Revolutionary Guards Corps-Qods Force have engaged in joint military training exercises. These paramilitary operations have included joint exercises with the Colombian guerrilla groups. This revolutionary guard is considered to have a well organized program capable of organizing a series of plans aimed at attacks against several specific targets at one time. Their selection process to conduct these attacks will depend on specific developments that alert to the successful completion of each assignment. This capacity for mobility around the world has been networked throughout the years establishing relations with nations that are willing to risk their national security in exchange for a global role in the transnationalization of terrorist activities. The targets are at a disadvantage, if for example, the elite guard decided to activate several terrorist cells at the same time. Warnings from Hugo Chavez indicate his intention to create several Viet Nam scenarios for the USA at the same time. This elementary tactic to divide and conquer would weaken the national defense of any nation, including the USA, allowing an invading force to create massive amounts of destruction in very little time. In addition, we still keep in mind that in 2009-2010 Venezuela also conducted military exercises with Russia off the coast of Florida.

The circle closes in when we take time to figure out the issue of Gangrillas. The training received by the guerrilla groups throughout Latin America, and around the world, would not provide the sufficient manpower to create an army capable of fighting against the United States Armed Forces. This asymmetrical war, however, could engage the gangs throughout Latin America and the USA to train under the direction of revolutionary groups throughout the world. We have been able to address how the guerrillas in Latin America have engaged in paramilitary training and assistance. We have also identified the presence of Hezbollah throughout Latin America, creating financial havens through which money laundering allows the financial solvency to support any terrorist enterprise. The financial support to provide the training, manpower and armament against the USA has been made a reality thanks to the American appetite for illegal drugs.

The Colombian Cartels, as we have known them for over three decades, are in their final hour as a national threat to Colombia. The "pentiti" tactics provided Colombia with quality intelligence gathering to penetrate the guerrilla's nests. Our believe that the illegal drug trade, and the violence linked to the narcoguerrillas has been resolved will cause the United States of America to wake up abruptly to the sound of AK-47's, ground to air missiles, and massive destruction created overnight by groups of **Gangrillas**. The level of terrorism these elements will bring into the USA is unparalleled to any other war American soldiers have fought in any foreign soil. One of the reasons we have succeeded at eliminating the head leaders of guerrilla groups in Latin America could possibly be because they were in direct confrontation with Hugo Chavez agenda to train the guerrilla groups with Russian, Chinese, Irish, and Islamic terrorist groups. In other words, the guerrilla group leaders served their purpose and had to be eliminated.

Guerrilla leaders were in juxtaposition to Chavez mandates, as each revolutionary group operated with an idealist leader focused on the assumption that their efforts would result eventually in leadership roles of presidential or dictatorship levels after their revolutionary movement succeeded. Courting and inviting the guerrilla groups into Venezuelan soil was first considered a joint exercise in which guerrillas would become part of the Bolivarian War, each leader assuming power in their own territory, and eventually fulfilling positions like Daniel Ortega achieved in Nicaragua. This would meet Chavez military goals under the Bolivarian War to have hemispheric unity with "one nation with many presidents." The transnationalization process networked through Hugo Chavez is aimed, however, at marching troops into the USA under the leadership of Hugo Chavez, President of the Bolivarian Republic of the Western Hemisphere. This title was dreamed of by the illustrious leader Simon Bolivar, which Chavez believes to have reincarnated.

It seems like gang leaders in the USA were recalled to Mexico in 2009 to receive new instructions, following a new mandate. This mandate, we assume after observing the recent cartel war in Mexico, may have included training exercises with guerrilla groups, returning to create a subdivision of gang members into cells subordinate to an urban cell gang leader. This cell leader must be accountable to other group leader, establishing a chain of command similar to soldiers, platoon leaders, and military chain of command/rank. Take into consideration the possibility that the guerrilla leaders in Latin America, similar to the "pentiti" program in Italy, may have options to engage in the Bolivarian War, or face extinction. Colombian and USA military operations have received valuable information leading to achieve the goals against guerrilla leaders. The ultimate break down will be determined by the mass of nearly twenty thousand Colombian guerrillas. Their choices will force them to reintegrate themselves to society through a process of restructuring their skills before reintegration into society; or joining the ranks of soldiers needed by the Bolivarian War under Venezuelan command. The guerrillas opting to the second choice will be providing training to the cadre of gangs throughout Latin America. Do you recall the Kuna Indian's and the Darien problematic, dealing with Colombian guerrilla groups visiting their land?

Central America has dealt with revolts, revolutions, and abrupt changes in government. The anti-government and revolutionary groups have become outcasts forced away from their nuclear families. Their families have been replaced by gang groups that invite the disgruntled and displaced into the criminal comfort of people sharing the same objectives. Failure of the Central American, and South American countries to reintegrate these subversive groups into society has nurtured the creation of groups of gangs that survive dealing and trafficking on illegal drugs. The criminality associated to these groups is a brutal degeneration created by militants without a cause. However, the degree of ruthlessness linked to the Mexican cartel's violent activity rises above most attacks perpetrated in the past. It could be that we have become insensitive to the plight of Latin American victims. It may also be an indicator that the globalization process now involves foreign cultural patterns that allow victimizing women, children, and the elderly to achieve terrorist goals. Although Latin American cartels and guerrillas have engaged in kidnappings, torture, and assassinations the emerging criminal patterns across the Mexican border are different.

Our apparent insensitivity to criminal activity happened as years went by listening to the Colombian cartel news of violence. Visiting Bogota in 2002 reopened the wounds, as the attacks against children were almost ignored by parents that had given up hope. The first thought in my mind was gratefulness for our right to bear arms. I felt confident that Americans would not have tolerated kidnapping of their children without giving up a fight. The circumstances we are facing are different since we are not facing native revolutionary groups. We are facing **Gangrillas**, isolated gang cells distributed throughout every state of the union. These groups have been trained with illegal drug profits under the leadership of terrorist groups. These terrorist groups have been successful in reintegrating themselves into communities across America, making it nearly impossible for law enforcement agencies to target their specific compounds, as they scatter in the middle of the day to hide in urban America.

Mexican Cartels have brought the Colombian war into our back door, and Arizona's frantic requests for assistance, as well as bordering states, from federal agencies and the National Guard are not exaggerated calls for help. The ruthlessness we are experiencing watching the Mexican dilemma develop across our border is the initial process of intimidation through undocumented ruthlessness. The massacre of seventy two illegal immigrants trying to enter the border is not even the tip of, not an iceberg, but a war of galactic proportions against American citizens. The message behind this attack against undocumented citizens from throughout the Western Hemisphere is the fate they will suffer if they fail to execute the mandates of the **Gangrillas**. I must remind you that these groups are not your average "West Side Story" gang members, but trained by a cadre of fundamentalist terrorists, whose alliance fall under Maoist beliefs, Islamic fundamentalist groups, and subversive groups whose only objective is to destroy the lifestyle enjoyed by the citizens of the United States of America. In addition, they may have received training from displaced KGB and Russian trained instructors to infiltrate America's infrastructure, weaken our democratic and capitalist system, and deteriorate the grounds that support our national system. The presence of displaced KGB Russian instructors working for the Russian Mafia in Mexican territory, support criminal elements responsible for magnifying the threatening levels of criminality and violence inching towards our porous border. All these groups have used illegal drug proceeds to fund their operations. The character, moral, and principles of these groups are in contradiction with our national values. Gangs trained by guerrillas, Islamic fundamentalist groups, and displaced Russian militants have aimed to use illegal drug dependence as a tool to further a political adventure. Recent reports in the news also indicate that these groups have infiltrated agencies in an effort to gather intelligence. Their objectives, as we continue to address, utilize illegal drug funds to advance their cause. Any city or town detecting gang symbols must heed to the warning signs.

The old cliché that **the future belongs to our children** will be used to close this segment. Last, but not least, detection of gang activities throughout our school systems must be taken seriously by school superintendents and principals, as they must create a solid partnership with law enforcement agencies. Fear that a school will be labeled as an unsafe institution must be put aside while having the courage to control the problem. Criminality covered up by our educational centers to protect "the image" of the school and its community has served to prevent law enforcement agencies from enforcing the law to protect the innocent victims that continue to be exposed to gangs, addicts and criminality. Respect for the integrity of a good administrator will always result in community support, as honesty and trust are still among the qualities that parents expect from school leaders. Our children must be comforted and reassured that we will stand together to protect their right to a better future.

CONCLUSION

In October 2010, Fidel Castro announced that fifty years of his communist revolution made him realize his system was a failure, and communism did not work. He would dismiss half a million, 500,000 workers because his system could not support them any longer. In the 1980's Castro also opened the gates to an invasion of the USA thorough the Marielita's port. Only military personnel called to control the invasion recognized Fidel's actions as an "on your face" invasion without any visible weapons but the effort to infiltrate American communities. These individuals, as expected under Castro's military strategy, were relocated across the USA to prevent the collapse of Florida's economy under a forced welfare emergency. The summer of 2011 will bring the second invasion of the USA, this time with collusion from Cuban and Russian agents, Colombian guerrillas, and the most feared fundamentalist terrorist groups. All subsidized by the American appetite for illegal drugs.

It is our hope that the facts an data presented throughout this book will provide you with the courage to make the right decision when you are called to cast a vote in favor or against legalizing drugs. Our conclusion is very clear throughout the analysis: this is a very complex network of incredible components, and the answer lies within the morals, principles, and strength of character of each individual. The most obvious has a tendency to become very confusing. National television broadcast of a two year old child smoking a joint of marihuana created uproar, while at the same time our nation remains silent at the marihuana prescriptions written to underage children by California doctors. Where do we draw the line?

Gangrillas have been trained by subversive revolutionaries with one objective in mind. The line will be drawn at the feet of every parent and the core of morals, principles, and values that identify their caliber as human beings. Embrace the thought that each reader will be called soon, and you need to be prepared to protect what you value the most. You will be called to make the right decision.

"A healthy mind in a healthy body" (Juvenal 55AD – 127 AD)

TERMINOLOGY

bazuco: processed cocaine of poor quality found in the Colombian area; lower quality of cocaine product

Bolivarización or Bolivarization: consolidation of power under the leadership of one individual that exhibits populist characteristics. Simon Bolivar's idea to unite the Latin American nations under one president was the original leader promoting Bolivarization.

Cocalero: coca leaf farmer

Coyote: term used when referring to human smugglers transporting illegal aliens through the Mexico-USA border.

de facto: concerning fact; actual; exercising power or serving a function without being legally or officially established; not founded upon law..

*de juro***:** concerning the law, by law; legitimate.

Drug bootlegger: drug dealer providing illegal drugs after the legalization process has been established.

ICITAP: International Criminal Investigative Training Assistance Program

IRGC-QF: Islamic Revolutionary Guards Corps –Quds Force

MAS: Muslim American Society, branch of the International Muslim Brotherhood

Narcoguerrillas: guerrillas involved in financing their revolutionary efforts and subversive movements through involvement with illegal drug trade or narcotraffic

Narcoterrorism: term used to indicate terrorist activities subsidized with financial profit through illegal drug trade or narcotics.

Narco-terrillas: symbiotic result of a process in which guerrillas that engage in narcotic trade acquire enough economic resources to engage in terrorist activities funded with narco-dollars.

pentiti: a person who forms part of a criminal or terrorist organization and after being arrested "repents" and decides to collaborate with the Judicial System in the investigations that involve his or her organization in exchange for benefits.

PHg's: Pot Home-growers

TBA: Triple Border Area that includes Paraguay, Uruguay and Brazil

USAG: USA Government

USADOJ: USA Department of Justice

WORKS CITED

Allison, Graham. (2009, Aug 9). "Graham Allison Calls for Citizen Follow-up to Countdown to Zero." Memorandum, **Harvard University, Belfer Center for Science and International Affairs**. Retrieved from http://belfercenter.ksg.harvard.edu/publication/20303/graham_allison_calls_for_citizen_followup_to_countdown_to_zero.html.

Allison, Graham. Graham. (2009, May 28). "Allison Commentary: North Korea won't fire nuke ... but could sell one to Osama." **The Sun: Harvard Kennedy School**. Retrieved from http://www.hks.harvard.edu/news-events/news /commentary/ north-korea-nuke-osama.

Argentina asks Interpol to Arrest Hezbollah leader (2002, October 1). *BBC Monitoring Original Source: Telam News Agency,* Buenos Aires. Retrieved from Global NewsBank database on April 30, 2007.

Artana, Daniel. (2010, Sept 2). "Why Banco del Sur is a bad idea." **Americas Quarterly:** *The Policy Journal for Our Hemisphere*. Retrieved from http://www. americasquarterly.org/artana-banco-del-sur.

Barros, Carolina. (2010, Aug 24). "Another Chinese conquest... or ... a Hugo Chavez "sellout" to Beijing." **VHeadline.com**. Retrieved from http://www.vheadline.com/readnews.asp?id=96037.

Bensman, Todd. (2008, Feb 7). "Iranians Plant Their Flag in Wilds of Nicaragua." **The New York Sun.** Retrieved on August 19, 2010 from http://www.nysun.com/ foreign/iranians-plant-their-flag-in-wilds-of-nicaragua/70934/.

"Brazil puts Mercosur-Israel free trade agreement on back burner." (2006, August 20). *BBC Monitoring Original Source: Correio Braziliense* web site, Brasilia. GNB April 30, 2007.

"Brazil says no indication of terrorist activity in Tri-Border Area." (2006, December 9). *BBC Monitoring Original Source: Ministry of Foreign Relations web site.* Retrieved from **Global NewsBank** database on April 22, 2007.

Byman, Daniel. "Should Hezbollah be next?" (2003, Nov/Dec). **Foreign Affairs** (Vol. 82, Issue 6, pp. 54-66). **Council on Foreign Relations.**

Callahan, Lauren. (2010, July 21). "Oakland city council approves large scale production of medical marijuana." **Oakland North.** Retrieved from http://oaklandnorth.net/2010/07/21/oakland-city-council-approves-large-scale-production-of-medical-marijuana/.

Carroll, Rory. (2010, Apri 27). "Iran's elite force expanding influence in Venezuela, claims Pentagon." **The Guardian.** Retrieved from guardian.co.uk.

Carter, Sara A. (2010, Jun 1). "Venezuela's Chavez backing leftist guerrillas in Mexico." *The Examiner. 1* Jun 2010. Retrieved August 15, 2010 from http://www.sfexaminer.com/world/Venezuela s-Chavez-backing-leftist-guerrillas-in-Mexico-95280089.html

Ceaser, Mike (2001, October 25). "Fears over 'tri-border' Islamic extremists." *BBC News.* Retrieved April 25, 2007 from http://news.bbc.co.uk/2/hi/americas/1617494.stm

"Coca cultivation and Cocaine Processing." **marihuanabusinessnews. com**. Retrieved from http://www.druglibrary.org/schaffer/govpubs/govpubs.htm

Connell, Curtis (2006, April 6). "Islam and the Global War on terrorism in Latin America." Event Transcript. **National Defense University**, Wash. D.C. Retrieved from http://www.pewforum.org.

Conway, Christopher.(2003) "Hugo Chavez and Bolivarian Nationalism." **The Cult of Bolivar in Latin American Literature**. UPF, FL.

De-Bourbon-Deuxi Siciles, Daniel. "The Politics of Hugo Chavez and the Bolivarian Revolution." **Associated Content News**. 13 Aug 2008.

Eland, Ivan. (1999, Oct 19) "Panama Canal Stirs Cold Warriors." **The Independent Institute Journal of Commerce**. Retrieved on July 2010 from http://www.independent.org/newsroom/article.asp?id=1067.

Faiola, Anthony (2001, October 13). "U.S. terrorist search reaches Paraguay." **The Washington Post Foreign Service**. P. A21.

Ferrand, Nicole M. (2009, Jan 29) "Terrorists buying Latin American Passports to enter the US?" **The Menges' Americas Report**. Retrievedon August 21, 2010 from the http://themengesproject.blogspot.com/2009/01/terrorists-buying-latin-american.

Fleischman, Luis. (2009, Jan 8). "Getting it right about the Chavez – Iranian Connetion." **The Menges Report**. Retrieved on August 22, 2010 from http://themengesproject.blogspot.com/2009/01/getting-it-right-about-chavez-iranian.html.

Forero, Juan. (2009, Nov 28). "Ahmadinejad boosts Latin American Ties." **The Washington Post. Retrieved from** http://www.washingtonpost.com/wpdyn/content/article/2009/11/27/AR2009112703130.

Gainor, Tim and Tiemoko Diallo. (2010 Jan). "Al Qaeda linked to rouge aviation network." **Reuters.** Retrieved from http://uk.reuters.com/article/idUSTRE60C3E820100113?sp=true

Gamboa, Suzanne (2006, October 16). "Lawmaker outlines intensifying border problems." *The Associated Press State and Local Wire.* LNA April 15, 2007.

Godnick, William H. (1998, Nov 10-11). "Illicit Arms in Latin America." **British American Security Information Council (BASIC).** Retrieved from http://sand.miis.edu/research/documents/gnick-osce.pdf.

Green, Eric (2006, May 1). "World's drug war intertwined with fighting terrorist groups." **State Department Documents and Publications.** LNA April 15, 2007.

Greenberg, Richard, A, and Stone Phillips Ciralsky. (2007, December 28). "Enemies at the gate." **NBC News.** Retrieved on August 22, 2010 from msnbc.com. http://rss.msnbc.msn.com/id/22419963/ns/dateline_nbc-international

Grey, M. and W. Sandholtz. (2003, Autumn). "International integration and national corruption." **International Organization** (Vol. 57, No. 4, pp. 761-800).

Haass, Richard N. (2010: Sept 8). "A Conversation with U.S. Secretary of State Hillary Rodham Clinton." **Council on Foreign Relations.** Retrieved from http://www.cfr.org/publication/22896/conversationwithussecretaryofstate hillaryrodham_clinton.html

Hall, Kevin (2007, April 8). "Reporter finds cracks in Mexico's port security." **The Sacramento Bee,** p. A1. Retrieved from Global NewsBank database on April 22, 2007.

Hanson, Stephanie. (2009, Aug 19). "FARC, ELN: Colombia's Left-Wing Guerrillas."**Foreign Affairs. Council on Foreign Relations.** Retrieved from http://www.cfr.org/publication/9272/farc_eln.html.

Heimann, F. and B. Heineman. (2006, May/ June). "The Long War Against Corruption." **Foreign Affairs. Council on Foreign Relations.** Retrieved from Global NewsBank database on April 16, 2007.

"Hezbollah offers to uproot corruption, evil in Venezuela." (2006, October 27). *BBC Monitoring Latin America: El Nacional.* LNA April 15, 2007.

Hudson, Rex (2003, July). "Terrorist and Organized Crime Groups in the Triple Border Area (TBA) of South America." *Library of Congress.* Retrieved April 25, 2007 from www.fas.org/irp/cia/product/frd0703.pdf

Johansmeyer, Tom. (2009, Nov 15). "First U.S. café opens for business in Portland." **DailyFinance.com.** Retrieved from http://www.dailyfinance. com/story/first-u-s-cafe-opens-for-business-in- portland/19239775/

"Latin America on alert for terror." (2004, August 25). *USA Today: World section.* Associated Press. Retrieved from Global NewsBank database on April 26, 2007.

"Latin Americans agree further details for Bank of the South. European Network on debt and development." (2010, July 2). Retrieved from http:// www.eurodad.org/whatsnew/articles.aspx?id=2494.

McDonnell, Patrick (2006, November 9). "Arrest Warrant issued for Rafsanjani in bombing." **Los Angeles Times: International and UN section.** Retrieved from Global NewsBank database on April 22, 2007.

"Mercosur: New intelligence force to operate in TBA." (2006, August 29). *Brazil Report.* **Intelligence Research Ltd.** LNA April 15, 2007.

Mittelstadt, Michelle (2006, October 17). "Border patrol, lawmen outgunned by cartels." *The Houston Chronicle*, p. A3. LNA April 15, 2007.

Molano, Walter T. (2008, Dec 12)."Bolivarian Dreams." **Latin Business Chronicles.**

Morton, Robert. 1999." Who needs the Panama Canal?" **World Tribune. com** Retrieved on Aug 22, 2010 from http://www.worldtribune.com/worldtribune/m-5.html.

No author. (2010, July 12). "Are we preparing for oil disruptions in the Gulf – the Persian Gulf?" *Catawissa Gazetteer.* Retrieved from http://catawissagazetteer.blogspot.com/2010/07/are-we-preparing-for-oil-disruptions-in.html.

No author. (2007, March 9). "Brazil politician charged with theft of over 11 million dollars." *Deutsche Press- Agentur.* Retrieved from Global NewsBank database.

Nye, Joseph Jr. (2005). **Understanding International Conflicts** (5th Ed.). New York: Pearson Education, Inc.

"OSAC: Overseas Security Advisory Council. Global Security News and Reports: Brazil 2009 Crime and Safety Report."(2009, Aug 27). **USDOS.** Retrieved from .https://www.osac.gov/Reports/report.cfm?contentID=106705

Perry, Frank. (2009: July 29) Interview: "Retired FBI agent: Terror suspects' arrests significant." **WRAL.com** Retrieved from http://www.wral.com/news/local/story/5676077/.

Peres de Oliveira, Vitoria (2006, April 6). "Islam and the Global War on terrorism in Latin America. Event Transcript." **National Defense University,** Wash. D.C. Retrieved from http://www.pewforum.org on April 26, 2007.

Pion-Berlin, David (2000, Spring). "Will Soldiers Follow? Economic Integration and Regional Security in the Southern Cone." **Journal on Interamerican Studies and World Affairs** (Vol. 42, No. 1, pp. 43-69).

Porter, Gareth (2006, November 18). "Argentina report casts doubt on Iran role in '94 bomb."**Inter Press Service.** Retrieved from Global NewsBank database on April 30, 2007.

Reel, Monte (2006, August 3). "Paraguayan smuggling crossroads scrutinized." **The Washington Post**, p. A16. Retrieved from Global NewsBank database on April 27, 2007.

Rojas, Carolina.(2008, Jan 13). "Inocentes Guerrilleros." **La Nacion.** Retrieved from http://www.lanacion.cl/prontus_noticias_v2/site/artic/20080112/pags/20080112154247.html

"Simon Bolivar: The South American Liberator." (2001, June 24). **Newsday Historical Digest**. 16.

Smith, Scott S. (2004) "Simon Bolivar: Liberator of Latin America." Retrieved from MilitaryHeritage.com.

Stecklow, Steve and Farnaz Fassihi. (2009, Sept 29). "Iran's Global Foray has Mixed Results." **The Wall Street Journal/ Economy.**

Sverdlick, Ana (2005). "Terrorists and Organized Crime Entrepreneurs in the Triple Frontier among Argentina, Brazil and Paraguay." **Trends in Organized Crime** (Vol. 9, No. 2, pp. 85-93).

The Compassionate Use Act of 1996. **The Medical Board of California**. Retrieved from http://www.medbd.ca.gov/medical_.html

Thomson, John (2006, August 21). "What Iranian Threat?" **National Review Online.** LNA April 15, 2007.

"Update 1-Roundup: Mercosur summit ends, pledging further regional integration." (2006, July 21). **Xinhua News Agency**. Retrieved from Global NewsBank on April 30, 2007.

Wagner, Richard. (2007, Jan 10) "Terror Connections Found in NC: FBI says most terror activity in the United States is of "non-violent" type." **Carolina Journal Online.** Retrieved from http://www.carolinajournal.com/articles/display_story.html?id=3816.

Webster, Michael. (2010, April 4). "Mexican drug cartels and terrorists are recruiting for more fighters to train as soldiers." **American Chronicle.** Retrieved on August 15, 2010 from http://www.americanchronicle.com/articles/view/58757.

BIOGRAPHIES

D. Mendez Beddow holds a Master of Arts in Liberal Studies from North Carolina State University (NCSU) since 1996 on International Affairs. She specialized on the issues related to narcotraffic in Latin America. Her experience includes consultant work for Plan Colombia and providing law enforcement instructor training throughout Latin America since 1992. She is a twenty year veteran educator in public schools.

Sam J. Thibodeaux has conducted research on terrorism, the South American Triangle Basin Area and Middle Eastern Affairs since 2000. Her research expertise provides crucial information needed for the transcontinental network analysis. She is a NCSU second generation graduate with a degree in Political Science and International Affairs. She also has second hand military experience married to a USA Army Afghanistan War veteran.